TESTIMO|

"The second I scanned the table of contents, I knew this book needed to be published! As a software developer and online marketer, I'm on the Internet every day. I know what dangers lay there.

As a grandparent, I know the dangers my grandkids face, and quite frankly it worries me. You can be sure that my daughter will be getting a copy of this book from me to help her protect my precious grandkids from the dangers lurking on the net every day.

Anyone with a child, grandchild, niece, or nephew needs this book now!"

Frank Sousa
www.trafficgeyser.com

"This is exactly the type of information that is needed for anyone online today to be safe. As the creators of a teenage social networking Website called MyHighSchoolLocker.com, we are very adamant about the online safety for our teenage members. The knowledge and content included in this book and the expert advice provided by Joyce and Preston having greatly improved the safety of our Website. We highly recommend this book to every parent looking to keep their children safer on the Internet."

Romeo Filip, CEO
www.MyHighSchoolLocker.com

"As a single dad and an attorney who focuses exclusively on Internet law, I highly recommend How to Protect Your Child Online. Get the book, read it right now, and apply what you learn to make your family safer."

Michael E. Young, Esquire
www.MikeYoungLaw.com

"I always say one of the best things you can do to further a relationship with someone else is to help your friend's children in some way, shape, or form. Well what better way can you help someone then sharing the book How to Protect Your Child Online? This book can protect children everywhere from all the dangers that await them online. Buy a copy for yourself and a few for your friends. Your friends will be glad you did."

Larry Benet, The Connector
www.LarryBenet.com

"How to Protect Your Child Online is a must-read for every parent whose child has access to the Internet—whether from their own desktop computer, laptop, or cell phone or from a friend's. Preston and Joyce offer clear, concise information and simple methods and techniques that teach parents how to teach their child to use the Internet safely. Their proactive, preventative approach of education and knowledge is a child's best defense against online predators. This book offers parents and children the opportunity to benefit from the vast learning and experiences the Internet offers while safely utilizing the technology. The tips on cyberbullying, chat rooms, instant messaging, social networking and sexual predators are priceless. The parenting tips for recognizing behavioral warning signs and the secrets for raising safe kids apply offline as well. I've given the book to my children so they can teach my grandchildren how to be safe online."

Judy Whalen, Founder, Providing resources that build character in kids and families.
ItStartsWithUs.com
ShopliftingIsStealing.com
StrengthenTheHarmony.com

"The book is a definite must for parents who care about having their children not become victims. Confidence building and creating a positive self-image are so very important in a child's life—in many respects and areas.

I especially liked the accuracy of the theme about children having confidence and a positive self-image. These cannot be overstated. In my experience of taking literally hundreds upon hundreds of robbery and other complaints as both a police officer and detective, most people who became victims looked and acted like victims. Suspects look for a person who looks like a victim because they just want to commit the offense and escape without being caught. The victims in many of the offenses normally lacked confidence: were old, young, timid, alone, etc., and the suspect saw an easy target. Suspects do not want aggression, confidence, confrontation, or flight, from a victim. Hit and run is their desired method."

Larry Powalisz
Career police officer, Coast Guard Intelligence

"Joyce and Preston have compiled a wealth of life-saving information in this valuable book. The instructions are clear and detailed; nothing is left to chance. I dream of the day all parents are required by law to read this book as soon as their pregnancy test is positive!"

Ellen C. Braun
www.RaisingSmallSouls.com

"A confident child stands a greater chance of developing into a healthy, productive, and independent adult. With many opportunities in the world today, as well as many risks, educating our children has become even more critical. Keeping Kids Safe provides the critical information for parents and educators to be informed and to educate our youth so that they will continue to be safe in the world, as they learn and grow. Joyce Jackson and Preston Jones are both a gift and a blessing, making sure we are equipped to prepare our youth for their future!

Wendy Darling
Thumbprints International
Creator of F.L.O.W. - U. Leadership Academy
and other programs for youth

"A powerful and insightful resource every concerned parent and caregiver must have in today's Internet-centric world. Joyce Jackson and Preston Jones deliver the in-your-face tough love I needed to learn the importance of Internet safety for my children. This book is filled with important techniques that show parents how to safeguard their children while empowering them with a vital education in self-reliance. Thank you, Joyce and Preston, for creating a powerful and easy-to-use resource for parents to protect their children."

JT DeBolt
www.ShiftOfMomentum.com

"As a father of two sons, ages seven and ten, who love to be on the Internet, I wondered if I was doing enough to protect them online. This book opened my eyes! It is chock-full of important information, resources, and techniques for parents to use to make a difference immediately. It will motivate you to become a better parent whether your child is online or not. Like myself, you will read the chapters over and over again and each time learn something new."

Robert Davila
Father

DON'T GET
PWNed!

HOW TO PROTECT
YOUR CHILD
ONLINE

BEST-SELLING AUTHORS
PRESTON JONES
& JOYCE JACKSON

New York

DON'T GET PWNed!

By Preston Jones & Joyce Jackson

© 2009 All rights reserved.

ISBN: 978-1-60037-520-0 (Paperback)

Library of Congress Control Number: 2008937050

Published by:

MORGAN · JAMES
THE ENTREPRENEURIAL PUBLISHER
www.morganjamespublishing.com

Morgan James Publishing, LLC

1225 Franklin Ave. Suite 325

Garden City, NY 11530-1693

800.485.4943

www.MorganJamesPublishing.com

Cover & Interior Designs by:

Johnson Design

Megan Johnson

www.Johnson2Design.com

Habitat
for Humanity®
Peninsula
Building Partner

In an effort to support local communities, raise awareness and funds, Morgan James Publishing donates one percent of all book sales for the life of each book to Habitat for Humanity.

Get involved today, visit:
www.HelpHabitatForHumanity.org

CONTENTS

Chapter 4

Chapter 5

Chapter 6

Chapter 7

Chapter 8

Chapter 9

Chapter 10

Chapter 11

Chapter 12

About Keeping Kids Safe

About the Authors

FOREWORD

The Internet has brought us many great advantages to modern life: information, connections across the globe, and new technologies that improve the possibilities and longevity of our lives.

At the same time, it has opened the doors to a whole new arena of danger no one could have envisioned just twenty short years ago. The threats to people who use the Internet are astounding. The predators and criminals online have far outpaced the knowledge and preventative measures we have all put in place.

As an Internet user myself, I am concerned about the way these criminals are spoiling the experience for me. As a parent, I am appalled at what they do behind anonymous keyboards and computer screens in search of their victims—kids.

There are many things we can do to stop these predators cold right now. Both collectively and individually we can take action to keep these people at bay and put them out of business and behind bars for a long time.

Step one for me, and I recommend for you, too, is to take a proactive, preventative approach to keeping yourself and your children safer online. Take charge of your child's and family's safety. Stay one step in front of the criminals.

The information is this book by Preston Jones and Joyce Jackson will enable you to do just that. Not only do you get information in a very clear, concise, easy-to-read format, you also get real skills, tips, and techniques you and your child can apply immediately to keep yourself safer online, right now, today, this instant.

True safety online comes from taking charge of your own safety and then teaching your child to do so as well. Relying on others to patrol and take care of the predators only works when they are constantly watching and patrolling every hour of the day. We know there are breakdowns in any system like that. We also know that we cannot expect our kids to be closely watched every second of every day of their lives and grow up to be independent, responsible adults.

Whether they are very young or a teenager, at some point in their life your children will be online. Modern life demands it, if not today, then tomorrow. They will need to know how to keep themselves safe because you will not always be there to protect them.

True, there are many computer and computer access screening software packages available. These monitor and block access to sites you do not want your child to view. There are also physical things you, as a parent, can do to protect them, such as forbidding your child online or watching them surf. However, what is really important is how will they be able to protect themselves when you are not around? What happens when they head off to college and have to get that paper done? Will they know what to look for in an online trap in order to avoid it? Will they know what to do if caught in one? Will they know how to be online to safeguard their identity and personal information?

It is true that not enough has been done to keep adults and children alike safe online. The early social network sites could not have

FOREWORD

anticipated how the predators would troll for kids on their pages. Nobody predicted phishing scams. At the same time, when faced with the fact that predators are a problem throughout their sites, most were slow, too slow, to respond. Some have refused to respond unless subpoenaed by the Federal government.

Stop waiting. Take action now. Today you have the opportunity to stop the predators from trapping members of your family. The manner in which the information is presented in this book is for busy parents, just like you, to scan in your free five minutes and then go home and easily implement it in your family.

The only flaw in this system is you if you fail to do it. Take action. Be one of the people who helps make the Internet safer not only for your family but for all of us.

INTRODUCTION

GETTING 'PWNed' IS BAD

"**I** just got PWNed!"

Is this Latin? French? Swedish? No, it is cyber-speak and your child, if they are online, uses it and knows how to speak it better than proper grammatical English.

Cyber-speak is a type of online shorthand that kids use in chat-rooms, emails and Instant Messages. There is a virtual dictionary full of A to Z terms in this cyber-speak language and one of the terms, "PWNed," is a negative thing. Getting "PWNed" is a put down and means you've been slammed, dissed, slapped, banned, stopped, pointed out as a dufus, and just about anything else that is derogatory that you can think of.

We don't want your child to get "PWNed" online. We're going to show you how to protect your child from this and other dangers while on the Internet. There's a lot of really great information out there on child safety online. We have great information for you, too. The difference with this book is we're going to give you the actual methods, what we call the How Tos and the Whys behind the infor-mation. This arms you and your child with a truly effective series of techniques to keep you both safer online.

There are many online dangers. For parents, the primary fear is about sexual predators hiding behind user names and passwords, masquerading as children or new friends and caring individuals. Everyone online, even adults, has to be careful. Everyone on the Internet needs to be armed with some safe surfing skills.

All of the ideas in this book are new. "New" means absolutely new, within the last ten years, twenty-first-century stuff. Nobody even fifteen or twenty years ago could have predicted just how criminals would infiltrate the World Wide Web. Right now, they are in the lead. The best we can do is react to the crimes and deeds they've committed. We have no proven way to completely stop them, as of this writing, except to stay out of their traps. On top of that, the Internet is still in its infancy. The projections as to how large, how worldwide, how prolific, and in what form the Web will be in just five years are astounding. What we do know is that we are only beginning to understand the Internet and how dangerous and threatening individuals can utilize it to prowl for victims. Moreover, kids are online more than ever. With younger kids online every day, the stakes are even higher.

Here's a piece of advice: if you think you and your family are safe because your children aren't allowed online, you are fooling yourself. Someday, they will be. At some point in their life, they will leave home and be on the Web. They had better know how to protect themselves while using it. We think today is a good day to start teaching them how to keep themselves safe online.

As a parent today, you have good reason to be afraid when your child is surfing the Web. However, you do not need to be ruled by that fear. Use it to motivate yourself to take action. The action is in taking charge as a parent of your child's safety online. You can actu-

INTRODUCTION

ally take charge of their online time, where they go, and how they handle situations that arise when they come across inappropriate material and individuals. Not only you as a parent, but also your child, can learn to be safer on the Web today. This book will show you how to do it.

Our approach to child safety is preventative. Preventing any type of child abuse is clearly preferable to resolving the emotional stress after a mistake has been made. We believe that parents can teach their children to spot potential dangers online and avoid them, with the help of our technique. If caught in a bad situation, they can get help and get out of it safely and securely.

One thing we must acknowledge is that the Internet is here to stay. It will be more accessible than ever in the next few years. Access will be available via an array of inexpensive handheld devices we can only dream of right now. The computer you have right now at home will be an antique. We believe it is better to be prepared than to be caught unaware.

The Internet, in our view, is a wonderful thing, although its use and reputation are being spoiled by the predators and criminals who use it for their nefarious deeds. The search engines, Web sites, and family-oriented information for anyone to find is phenomenal. However, let's not kid ourselves—the dangers online will grow. The predators are inventing new ways to entrap adults and children alike, almost daily.

We're going to stay one step ahead of them. We are providing this information to all who care about kids and kids being online safely.

We're going to shut the criminals down through education and preventative measures before our kids get entrapped in their schemes.

And, why this book, now?

Following the success of our first #1 best-selling book, *How to Protect Your Child from Sexual Predators,* we realized there is a need to address one of the biggest growing concerns of parents today: Internet safety.

Frankly, most parents today have little knowledge of the World Wide Web. As a matter of fact, their kids know more about it than they do. So this book will help any parent, like us, whose kids are savvier online than they are.

HOW THIS BOOK CAN HELP YOU

This book provides our effective tips and techniques for preventing online predators from catching and abusing any more kids, your kids.

For the criminal online, we're putting them on notice that they are out of business.

The first way this book will help you instantly is by educating you that the predators are online. It's a fact. They are hiding behind the anonymity of keyboards and usernames. They are lurking everywhere the kids hang out. They are trolling for victims.

This is frightening. It is, however, powerful knowledge for you.

INTRODUCTION

In knowing this fact, you can learn how to stay one step ahead of them or better yet, avoid being trapped by them all together.

Apply the tips and techniques that are in this book. They are not rocket science, but easy and simple common sense solutions that are effective.

You can even use this book as a reference guide. Flip through the book, and pick a chapter that appeals to you or answers an immediate need. Read it. Then find another. Come back and flip through the easy bullet point chapter summaries. Keep the book near your computer. Each chapter is written to stand on its own. Tear pages out and tape them to your child's computer.

It's all about your kids. It's about both them and you being safer online immediately as well as in the long-term. It's all about keeping them safe for their entire lifetime.

CHAPTER 1

MY CHILD IS NOT ALLOWED ONLINE! AND OTHER SAFETY MYTHS

THE 7 PITFALLS OF IGNORANCE ONLINE

"**W**ell, I hear what you are saying, but this doesn't apply to me. My child is not allowed online!"

Whenever we hear this indignant, righteous response from parents, our first reaction is, "OK. Good for you." Then we go into another room and just shake our heads. The children of these parents are at greater risk from online predators and abuse at some time in their life than those who are currently allowed online.

Shocked?

Sometimes we also hear, "My child's safe. I have the computer in the living room so I can see what they are doing and where they go online." We shake our heads some more.

The latest report from the National Center for Missing and Exploited Children, in 2006, reports:

- About fourteen percent of the youths online (ten to seventeen years old) received a sexual solicitation or approach over the Internet.

HOW TO PROTECT YOUR CHILD ONLINE

- Four percent (4%) received an aggressive sexual solicitation—a solicitor who asked to meet them somewhere; called them on the telephone, or sent them offline mail, money, or gifts.

- Thirty-four percent (34%) had an unwanted exposure to sexual material—pictures of naked people or people having sex.

- Twenty-seven percent (27%) of the youth who encountered unwanted sexual material told a parent or guardian. If the encounter was defined as distressing—episodes that made them feel very or extremely upset or afraid—forty-two percent (42%) told a parent or guardian.[1]

The Pew Internet and American Life Project report on the Internet determined that one in three American children have been cyberbullied.[2] *Girlfriend Magazine* reported in April, 2006, that 42 percent of Australian teens have been cyberbullied and along with this, two more disturbing facts:

- Girls are two and a half times more likely to be victims of cyberbullying.

- Girls are more likely to be cyberbullies.[3]

As for adults, the parents of these children, nearly one in five adults have fallen victim to an Internet scam, as reported by a Microsoft survey in August of 2007.

You can do a lot as a parent to make sure your child is not one of these victims at some time in their life. It is not, however, done by forbidding them to go online.

Why?

CHAPTER 1

MY CHILD IS NOT ALLOWED ONLINE!

If you forbid them to go online, we can almost guarantee you that at some time before they are eighteen years of age, they will do so when you are not around. They had better be prepared. If you don't prepare them to be online at some point in their lives, regardless of whether they are today or not, you are committing one of the 7 Pitfalls of Ignorance Online. This attitude, if you hold it, is putting your child at great risk.

The truly safe child online is one who is armed with information on how to safely surf the Web. This information is useful to anyone with kids, whether you allow them online on not. Education and knowledge are your most powerful tools. The following tips are even appropriate for most adults as we all negotiate our way through life.

Want to know one of the easiest ways to be safer online immediately? Avoid these seven pitfalls:

PITFALL #1: "MY CHILD IS NOT ALLOWED ONLINE!"

Most kids will, during their lifetime, get online whether you allow it or not. In today's world, your child will be at school, at the library, in a museum, or at a friend's house and invariably find themselves with access to the Internet. School projects, classes, advanced research, and other necessary information-gathering tasks will someday be necessary for your child to do on the Internet.

They need to be prepared and you are the one who must prepare them.

It's that simple. Knowledge and education are very powerful tools for a lifetime of safety. Even a young adult doing advanced research online as a college student needs to be trained in Internet safety.

You can forbid your child to be online right now, and as a parent that is your right. We suggest, however, that you at least mentally prepare them with the facts about *why* they are not allowed online. You can talk to them about it in age-appropriate terms and share with them your ideas and fears about online safety.

PITFALL #2: "I HAVE THE COMPUTER IN THE LIVING ROOM, SO I CAN WATCH WHAT THEY ARE DOING."

One of the biggest things we know is that safety, especially teen safety, springs from a basis of trust and self-confidence. If you want to keep the computer somewhere you can see it while your children are young, that is OK and your choice. You can also choose to move the computer into the living room, but we encourage you to educate your child not only about how the Internet works, but also why the computer is sitting where it is.

Your ability to constantly police your children's actions only goes so far. When they are on their own at some point, you will not be there to make choices for them. They need to learn to make sound choices for themselves, and this includes their online safety.

Tell them, in age-appropriate words, what the dangers are: sexual predators, cyberbullies, traps, and scams. Be honest and share your thoughts and feelings with them. You can do this without creating fear and paranoia.

Include in the discussion safety tips and rules as you foster trust and respect between you and your child with frank discussions about the Internet. Explain to them why the computer is located where it is. It may be the most practical furniture configuration, or an "it's the only place it can go" location issue. Tell them that. It may be that you want to watch them while they're online. Tell them that, too. The Internet is great fun, but it's also a haven for criminals and childhood dangers.

The point is, talk to your child about what you are thinking and doing with the computer and the Internet. Be honest and up-front with what you say. If you are afraid, it is OK to tell them this. Set the basis for an honest, up-front relationship with your younger children. With older kids, continue a relationship of trust and respect-building. Tell them if you are not really knowledgeable about the Web. Also tell them about your joys or fears of having them on it. Tell them it's not a lack of trust in them, just a matter of safety that is the basis of your concerns.

Here's a novel idea: have them educate you, too. Most teenagers and older kids know more about computers than their parents. Have them tell you about the Internet and what they find there. Have them tell you what they see and perceive. This healthy exchange gives you, as their parent, a better understanding of their perspective of the Web.

You can both do this in a conversational way, too. There is enough fear and paranoia in the world. The Internet does not need to add more to it. Yes, being online can be a dangerous place for kids, so educate your child as to those dangers and how to avoid them. They can be aware of these issues, recognize them, and keep themselves out of harm's way.

PITFALL #3: "THEY CAN ONLY CHAT WITH THEIR SCHOOL FRIENDS ONLINE."

If there is one thing to understand about the Internet and being safe online it is this: there is no "only" to it or on it. There is nothing that is privy to only one or two people online. Any and all information can be shared or surreptitiously stolen and used by anyone with ill intentions.

We love to tell kids that they must assume aliens on Jupiter are reading their online posts, emails, and instant messages. There are no "my friends only" and there is never, *never*, a one–on-one conversation on the Internet.

Also, be aware that if you allow your child to email and chat with only school friends, their chats may be monitored by others. Always work from a perspective that nothing is private on the Web.

The other danger online from school friends is cyberbullying— mean and vicious bullying between kids in the form of emails, instant messages, and postings. Friends, peers, and school acquaintances are notorious for engaging in cyberbullying. Confident children who understand that their parents and family are there for them can deflect,

MY CHILD IS NOT ALLOWED ONLINE!

delete, and ignore cyberbullying more effectively. They may even be able to oust the bullies from the group or independently decide they want to leave a chat group or email chain because they want better friends in their lives.

PITFALL #4: "I KNOW THE PERSON ON THE OTHER END IS EXACTLY WHO THEY SAY THEY ARE."

Unless the person you are interacting with online is a close family member, trusted friend, or confirmed colleague, always maintain skepticism that new contacts or chat room friends are who they say they are. We are not encouraging paranoia; however, we are suggesting that a healthy skepticism is good. It is too easy for anyone to hide anonymously behind keyboards and usernames. Relationships, even cyberfriends, take time to develop. Take the time; never assume anything is absolutely true in new relationships formed on the Internet, and make the new friends prove beyond a doubt they are who they claim to be.

If you have young children or teenagers, never allow them to accept gifts from anyone they meet online. If they do, make sure you personally have talked to the person on the telephone. It's a good idea to review the email correspondence, too. You must have one hundred percent confidence that the people are who they say they are before you ever let your child interact with them on a personal level.

Additionally, never allow your child to meet anyone in person they met first online unless you are confident in that meeting and relationship. If you do agree to let your child meet a new cyberfriend, go with them to that meeting and make sure it takes place in a highly populated, public place.

PITFALL #5: "I KNOW EVERYONE ONLINE VIEWS MY PICTURES AND PHOTOS OF MY KIDS AS I DO."

The lesson here is, only you and your immediate family believe your child is the cutest thing on the planet today. It's a pretty healthy view to have when online, too. All parents want the world to know how beautiful their children are. Many teens want others to know how attractive they are. Young singles looking to meet a mate want to entice potential candidates with photos.

Photo sites, sites where kids play and hang out, teen sites, and social networks are all places attractive to sexual predators. It is a fact that predators hang out where they know their prey will be. They are quietly, secretly lurking on all the sites the kids are on. Why do you think there are laws in every state mandating the distance a convicted sexual offender must live from the boundary of children's schools? Simple: predators hang out where the kids are. It makes most parents uncomfortable to read this, but it is true. Knowing this fact will help you keep your child safer online.

Predators go where the kids and materials they need are easily accessed. And what is one of the materials they need? They need photos of kids, teens, and other potential victims. They search for

MY CHILD IS NOT ALLOWED ONLINE!

photos of victims and create lurid dreams by downloading, sharing, and printing them. These individuals use your child's photos differently than you do.

While it's a terrific rule to never upload a picture of your child to the internet, we know photo sites are here to stay. Parents and families will always want to boast about their handsome children. Just be smart. Be aware.

PITFALL #6: "EVERYONE ONLINE SHARES THE SAME INTENTIONS I HAVE WHEN I'M ONLINE."

You must always assume that every new person you meet online has absolutely different intentions from yourself. It does not necessarily mean they are evil; it just means they are different from you, and you need to be aware of that fact.

We have an advantage when we meet someone new face-to-face. We can sense something about them that tells us if we want to interact with them further or not. Without our innate ability to look at, interact personally with, and "size up" a new friend with our senses, we need to be extra cautious in assuming that everyone we meet online is as well-intentioned as we are.

More than that, the fact is, many people lack good written communication skills today, and it is just too easy to misunderstand even the simplest of emails. The old adage, "Better safe than sorry" definitely holds true here. Unless you know someone very well, never assume they are just as well-intentioned as you.

PITFALL #7: "PREDATORS ONLINE FIND US AND MY CHILD BY CHANCE."

Criminals and sexual predators do not work all day, shop at the store on the way home, eat dinner, and then troll for victims in their spare time at night before going to sleep.

Finding victims is their full-time job. Not only that, they are very driven in their focus to find victims. They create and invent new ways of surreptitiously trapping and winding in their victims like fish on a line. They will be very patient as their trap unfolds and ensnares you or your child.

Why are we telling you this?

Parents need to be aware of what they are dealing with online. If you understand it, then you can understand why it is better to implement preventative safety measures that make you and your child safer than to become a victim lamenting," I never thought it would happen to me." Stay one step ahead of the predators. Be cautious. You have no normal human instincts to rely upon when you are online because you cannot relate person-to-person with people behind keyboards.

Our advice is, be cautious, be careful. Understand that you and your child are a target for full-time criminals bent on catching the both of you. The pitfalls of surfing the internet can be avoided with a little knowledge that can be applied every time you are online.

CHAPTER SUMMARY

The 7 Pitfalls of Ignorance Online

- **Pitfall #1:** "My child is not allowed online!"
- **Pitfall #2:** "I have the computer in the living room, so I can watch what they are doing."
- **Pitfall #3:** "They can only chat with their school friends on-line."
- **Pitfall #4:** "I know the person on the other end is exactly who they say they are."
- **Pitfall #5:** "I know everyone online views my pictures and photos of my kids as I do."
- **Pitfall #6:** "Everyone online shares the same intentions I have when online."
- **Pitfall #7:** "Online predators find us by chance."
- Our advice is, be cautious, be careful. Understand you and your child are a target for full-time criminals bent on catching the both of you. The pitfalls of surfing the internet can be avoided with a little knowledge that can be applied every time you are online.

CHAPTER 2
WHY USING THE WEB IS NOT LIKE USING A CELL PHONE

HOW A LITTLE KNOWN SECRET CAN HELP YOU AND YOUR CHILD BE SAFER ONLINE IMMEDIATELY

If there is any one thing you can do to keep your children safe online, no matter what their age, it is to educate them. We believe kids, when given the right knowledge in words they understand, will follow the best practices and make the best choices for themselves. It's called empowerment.

Empowering your child is essential. And the one fact, the one little secret to empowering and educating your child about the Internet right now is: *the web is not a cell phone!*

Most kids, teens especially, are very cell phone savvy. They grew up using them and have a knowledge of them that far outstrips most parents'. Almost any teenager can flip open a phone with one hand and flick an answer key with a deft thumb when the custom ringtone goes off. Adults, on the other hand, have to fish phones off of belts or out of a pockets and purses. We carefully open them with two hands and push the answer button with an index finger while squinting at the keypad. Any major numbers to be dialed had better be keyed into the phonebook since our sausage-like fingers tap more than one key at a time.

While it's a funny image, it leads to the real point: our kids use cell phones with great skill and expertise to chat with their friends one-on-one. They literally grew up with them and are very skilled in using them as a regular part of their daily routine. Regardless of their dexterity, kids chat anywhere, anytime with friends they have personally given out their cell phone number to. They can say anything they want to any friend just as if they were in the same room together, face-to-face. It's instant gratification for kids who want immediate access to friends to gossip.

Parents have encouraged this behavior because the cell phone has been an easy and comforting way to stay in touch with any child who is out of sight. Cell phones afford us a measure of control as parents through instant communication with our children. It is a convenience of our culture and times which parents and children alike barely give a thought to.

Approaching the Internet in a manner similar to cell phones is dangerous. Kids assume what they do online is one-on-one, just as if it were a natural offshoot of the cell phone. You can't blame them; they have no idea. Parents don't either.

Always assume everything—and we mean absolutely everything—you do online is being viewed, copied, recorded, and shared with everyone else online. Assume that millions and millions of us-

CHAPTER 2

WHY USING THE WEB IS NOT LIKE USING A CELL PHONE

ers around the world will see your post, email, personal information, and anything you have to say about Aunt Jennie or your friend Kurt. Assume it all is or will be made public.

You had also better assume that there are nefarious individuals around filled with ill intent, yes criminals, everywhere you go on the Internet. They are bent on spying on your personal online communications to snare their victims. They do it everyday, and you need to know this in order to be safer online.

Do you know what else?

If you talk to your children about this fact, they understand it. If you teach them that anytime they are online, they are not alone or one-on-one with their friend, they get it. Watch how wide their eyes get at the moment they understand what you are telling them. If you are technically inclined, tell them how the information is electronically passed around. You may even want to show them with your computer.

Everything that appears on the Web can be downloaded, traced, or stolen. The Pentagon's secure computer system has been hacked over the years. Why would you think your personal information or computer at home is private?

If you discuss the ramifications of being so public with private thoughts, pictures, and information with your kids in terms they can understand, they will not only recognize the problem, they will be willing participants in the solution as well. Most teens equate chatting online and sending emails to friends with using a cell phone. They perceive it as a private conversation. If you discuss with them the realities of the Internet and what solutions they can use to avoid being trapped by predators who are intentionally masquerading as friends, they will start to do several concrete things to be safer on their own.

THE POWER OF KNOWLEDGE

Knowledge is power. This is no news or revelation from a safety standpoint. Most true safety stems from simple, common sense principles. Explaining to teenagers that everything they see and do online bounces off satellites, electronic waves, and optic cables around the world gets their attention. Explaining how someone in Sydney chatting online with a friend down the block can easily be seen by someone in Milan, makes them think.

Depending on the age of your children, it may also be a good idea to let them know that there are certain people out there that they need to avoid. Predators hang out where kids do. Predators trolling for victims go where they can find them. Your children, in very simple terms, need to know there are certain individuals online who mean them harm. Telling them these things, of course, is your decision as their parent. We encourage you to think seriously about it, though. When kids understand, really understand, the whys behind every rule they must follow, they get out of the realm of, "Mom and Dad are making me do this," into, "Wow! How about that!" It leads to them becoming involved in sticking to the rule, too. They assume some ownership in their own safety. Assuming that your children are intelligent and respecting their intelligence goes very, very far in personal online safety.

Younger children can get this too. When expressed in terms that are age-appropriate, even younger kids, kids who head to sites to play math or vocabulary-building games recommended by teachers, can begin to understand how to safely navigate the Internet.

I NEVER THOUGHT IT WOULD HAPPEN TO ME

We've probably scared the heck out of most of you by now. Good. The idea is that you have to be very, very aware and cautious to stay one step ahead of the dangers online because of the anonymity afforded everyone there. We sincerely want to help you and your children keep out of the traps being set for you online.

The one theme that comes through all the crime statistics, all the surveys and studies done on crime victims, is this: "I never thought it would happen to me." When parents follow this line of thinking, it means they have not been thinking. It means they have been lazy or naïve or both. It means they have not prepared themselves for real life.

Just because you prepare yourself against the dangers online does not mean anything bad will happen. It does not mean you are inviting criminal behavior. On the contrary, the things in this book take just minutes a day to implement for a lifetime of safe online surfing. It just means you are prepared. It's like buckling your seat belt every time you get into a car. You buckle up for safety, but you don't wish for a car accident. Be prepared.

CHAPTER SUMMARY

- If there is any one thing you can do to keep your children safe online, no matter what their age, it is to educate them.

- Education empowers your children to take responsibility for their safety online.

- The one fact, the one little secret in educating your children about the internet immediately is: THE WEB IS NOT A CELL PHONE!

- Using the Internet in a way that mimics cell phones is dangerous.

- Always assume everything, and we mean absolutely everything, you do online is being viewed, copied, recorded, and shared with everyone else online.

- You and your children are targets for anonymous and hidden dangers online. Awareness of this fact will keep you safer, more secure, and hopefully, out of the traps that snare the unaware surfing the World Wide Web.

- Everything that appears on the Web can be downloaded, traced, or stolen.

CHAPTER 3

THE 21ˢᵀ CENTURY DANGERS OF THE INTERNET

OUTSMARTING THE FULL-TIME CRIMINALS

We wake up, get up in the morning, eat breakfast with the family, dress the kids for school, head out for work, spend our day making a living, come home at night, have dinner, and spend an hour doing one or two things before we go to bed.

There are work pressures, family demands, shopping, maintenance around the yard and other things we have to do. There are many things we want to do as well. The day ends; we sleep. Tomorrow, we will get up and do it again.

So do the criminals and predators online, right?

Wrong!

Trolling for victims, setting traps, and reeling in unsuspecting individuals is a full-time endeavor, a full-time job so to speak, for the criminals online. Unless you understand this, you don't have a prayer for keeping your child safe online. You don't have a prayer for prevention and staying one step ahead of them, unless you understand you are up against people who spend their entire day looking for prey. To stay out of their traps, you need advice and expertise. That is where we come in.

You can stay one step ahead of them with the information in this book. On top of that, develop a proactive approach to your child's online safety. Be aware of the dangers and how predators work. By knowing just how they try to trap you and how they've trapped victims in the past, you can become armed with a very powerful knowledge. This knowledge will allow you to keep both you and your child safer online. It's called, "outsmarting the full-time criminals."

CYBERBULLYING

Bullying is not new. It probably was around with Og and the other cavemen. Bullying is a negative part of human nature. Its prevalence is startling:

- Bullying is the most common form of violence in our society; between 15 percent and 30 percent of students are bullies or victims.

- A recent report from the American Medical Association on a study of over 15,000 6th–10th graders estimates that approximately 3.7 million youths engage in, and more than 3.2 million are victims of, moderate or serious bullying each year.[4]

- Between 1994 and 1999, there were 253 violent deaths in school; 51 casualties were the result of multiple death events. Bullying is often a factor in school-related deaths.[5]

- Membership in either bully or victim groups is associated with school drop out, poor psychosocial adjustment, criminal activity, and other negative long-term consequences.

- Direct, physical bullying increases in elementary school, peaks in middle school, and declines in high school. Verbal abuse, on the other hand, remains constant. The U.S. Department of Justice reports that younger students are more likely to be bullied than older students.

- Over two thirds of students believe that schools respond poorly to bullying, with a high percentage of students believing that adult help is infrequent and ineffective.

- Twenty-five percent of teachers see nothing wrong with bullying or putdowns and consequently intervene in only 4 percent of bullying incidents.[6]

Cyberbullying, or bullying someone via the Internet, is a twenty-first century phenomenon, but it should not be a surprise to you.

Cyberbullying is simply a child being targeted by someone with bad intentions through email, chat rooms, or instant messaging. It is just like offline bullying, only delivered digitally and includes harassing, tormenting, threatening, or embarrassing someone through online messages.

It's usually kid to kid, but sexual predators either watch and enjoy the exchanges for the thrill or may join in, disguising themselves as children and thus adding to the danger. Regardless, it is destructive and nasty.

DON'T GET PWNed!

If adults do join in and bully children, it becomes harassment. Adults online harassing children becomes cyber-harassment. If the offending adult chases kids online, it turns into cyber-stalking. The good news is, these adults can be criminally prosecuted.

But with kids, what is the problem with cyberbullying?

Cyberbullying provides nothing but negative results for the victim. It does not feel good and lowers self-esteem. It can also escalate into physical violence. We've all heard the sensational news stories about children who have killed each other or committed suicide after having been involved in a cyberbullying incident.

While cyberbullying can consist of a single incident, it typically involves several messages over a period of time. Kids usually know it when they see it. They spot it immediately. Parents, on the other hand, may have a hard time recognizing it and dismiss it as a one-time thing. They also tend to worry more about the lewd language used by the kids rather than the negative effects of the rude and embarrassing posts.

When your child is a victim of cyberbullying, you can take action. First, let you child tell you about it. Let him share his emotions and feelings about the incident. Let him talk; just stay quiet and listen. Let him release his feelings in his own words. It is a very good way to enable him to let go of the pent-up emotions about what is occurring.

Second, teach your child to "count to five." This means, show her how to take a deep breath, put down the mouse, and calm down. Most cyberbullying continues because it is a back and forth, give and take exchange of messages. In many cyberbullying cases, the bully becomes the victim as the exchange continues or more kids become involved. Victim and bully often exchange places. A great way to stop it is to teach your child to count to five, put down the mouse, move away from the computer, and stop the exchange.

Third, if the cyberbullying comes from a group of kids at a particular school, which much of it does, get the school and the students involved in putting a stop to it. Get involved in the solution as a caring parent of a student. A school's involvement in terms of educating the kids is critical to stopping the cyberbullying. Teaching the students about the negative effects and consequences of bad cyber manners gets them personally involved in owning the problem and solving it. You could even help by being a part of the school assemblies and pamphlets that may be needed in the education process.

Schools can be very effective in educating students on cyberbullying, online ethics, and Internet courtesies. They may be able to provide additional help like setting up an anonymous method of reporting cyberbullying. Administrations can receive these anonymous tips and take quick, appropriate action to shut down the site or remove the cyberbully.

Again, involve the students, involve the school, and maintain a presence as a concerned parent. Kids need to know that they can create their own campaign to help put an end to cyberbullying entirely. Empowering the kids to implement their own solution is critical.

IDENTITY THEFT

When we talk about identity theft online, we are talking primarily about your financial identity being stolen. If your child has a social security number, or your teenager a bank account or credit card, they, like you, are at risk when online. The following safety tips can help both you and your child.

Just how prevalent is identity theft?

A survey conducted by the Federal Trade Commission (FTC) in 2006 estimated that 8.3 million American consumers, or 3.7 percent of the adult population, became victims of identity theft in 2005. Most of the financial losses are suffered by credit issuers and banks. Victims are rarely held responsible for fraudulent debts incurred in their name. However, victims often bear the responsibility of contacting their banks and credit issuers after an identity theft has occurred. The same FTC survey determined that victimized consumers spent over 200 million hours in 2005 attempting to recover from identity theft.[7]

First of all, just what are we talking about in stealing an identity? Primarily, we mean your financial identity:

- Name
- Address
- Social security number
- Mother's maiden name
- ATM PIN Number

THE 21ST CENTURY DANGERS OF THE INTERNET

- Date of birth
- Bank account number

Other information can be involved, but these are the typical pieces of information stolen and used regularly in identity theft.

The next step in preventing identity theft is in understanding just how this information is stolen. Many victims are shocked to learn that someone else has been taking out loans, getting cell phone accounts, acquiring new credit cards, and even committing crimes using their information.

Criminals collect pieces of identifying information about you and then piece them together to create a new you, that is, a second you. The real you has good credit. The other person pretending to be you is creating a huge amount of debt.

At the onset of the theft, you have no idea the second version of yourself exists. To add insult to injury the thief's real name and identity are invisible because the thief uses your name and identity. Unfortunately, unless they have already been victimized, most adults do not pay serious attention to identity theft. This phenomenon is not even on most teenager's or young adult's radar screen.

We want you to be aware of what could happen. We want you to be prepared. Be safe online and free from identity theft. Again the way to do this is through education and prevention. Here's what you can do:

- Limit the number of identification cards that you have.

- Investigate the online Websites you shop at and understand their security measures.

- Refuse to give out personal information online unless you have initiated the purchase.

- Refuse to give out personal information over the phone unless you have initiated the call.

- Sign up for the State or National Do Not Call Registry.

- Shred or destroy credit card receipts, credit applications, bank checks, and financial statements.

- Regularly review your credit card and other financial statements.

- Order and review a copy of your credit report.

THE FUTURE OF THE INTERNET AND OTHER UPCOMING SURPRISES

So, you've read this chapter; think you're prepared? What could the Internet possibly be like, even in the next few years so that we can be safer online? What can you expect?

The Technology & Democracy Project out of Washington, D.C. estimates that in the U.S. alone, Internet traffic will grow fifty-fold by 2015.[8] We stay on top of the Internet as best we can so we stay one step ahead of the dangers. As the Internet expands, predators and criminals will be inventing new ways to stalk and troll for your child, so we will stay on top of how they operate in order to give you tools and skills to avoid them.

CHAPTER 3

THE 21ST CENTURY DANGERS OF THE INTERNET

In the meantime, we love the Internet! It is a fascinating and exciting place to be. Here's just a smattering of what we can expect to see in the near future.

Digital information will be available in more immediate ways. Even television will be delivered over the Web. Visionary Bill Gates of Microsoft said in a speech in 2007 that he believes more and more viewers will abandon traditional television over the next five years. He thinks they will trade television's fixed program times and advertisements for the flexibility offered by online video.[9]

As for the capacity of the Web and some mandated controls on digital information and video, it looks like it might be coming. Right now, online video is untethered. There are no controls over anything uploaded for viewing or how many times it's uploaded, let alone how it's named and tagged. This continuing flood of new video and other Web content could overwhelm the Internet by 2010 unless providers invest big time, up $137 billion has been the estimate,[10] in new internet capacity.

The mobile phone or PDA you now have looks like it just might change everything. We know there is a push with mobile device makers towards better looking interfaces, better quality cameras, super fast processors and extra long life batteries.

Just coming to terms with Web 2.0? Web 3.0 is a new term used to describe the future of the Web. Many technology leaders have used the term Web 3.0 to talk about a future wave of Internet innovation.

Web 3.0 is supposed to deliver a new generation of information and business applications. This means "on demand" information will be customizable and available for both business and consumer needs. It will radically change many major groups, companies, and organizations and how they work. It will change the nature of careers and jobs.

New ways of delivering all this customizable content will appear. Some are in beta testing now. Examples today are the various RSS aggregators such as Yahoo Pipes.

What all this means is a very exciting, dynamic way of life that we must prepare ourselves and our children for. Education and safety on the Internet are our goals.

CHAPTER SUMMARY

- Cyberbullying, or bullying someone via the Internet, is a twenty-first century phenomenon.

- Cyberbullying is simply a child being targeted by someone with bad intentions through email, chat rooms, or instant messaging.

- Adults online harassing children becomes cyber-harassment. If the offending adult chases kids online, it turns into cyber-stalking.

- Cyberbullying usually occurs over a period of time.

- If your child is a victim of cyberbullying, you can take a number of actions. One, let your child tell you her emotions and feeling about the incident. Two, teach your child to count to five. Three, if the cyberbullying comes from a group of kids at a particular school, which much of it does, get the school involved.

- The kids themselves can create their own campaign to help put an end to cyberbullying.

- When we talk about identity theft online, we are talking primarily about your financial identity being stolen. This includes your:
  - √ Name
  - √ Address
  - √ Social security number
  - √ Mother's maiden name
  - √ ATM PIN number

√ Date of birth

√ Bank account number

- Criminals collect pieces of identifying information about you and then piece them together to create a "new you."

- You have no idea the second version of yourself exists. Here's what you can do to help prevent your identity from being stolen:

    √ Limit the number of identification cards that you have.

    √ Investigate the online Websites you shop at, and understand their security measures.

    √ Refuse to give out personal information online unless you have initiated the purchase.

    √ Refuse to give out personal information over the phone unless you have initiated the call.

    √ Sign up for the State or National Do Not Call Registry.

    √ Shred or destroy credit card receipts, credit applications, bank checks, and financial statements.

    √ Regularly review your credit card and other financial statements.

    √ Order and review a copy of your credit report.

CHAPTER 4
INSTANT MESSAGING AND CHAT ROOMS ARE HERE TO STAY

WHAT YOU CAN DO:
TAKING THE ADVANTAGE, TAKING CHARGE

Can kids chat online safely? This is a topic that not only terrifies many parents, it also elicits smiles from many safety experts.

Smiles? Yes. It is something that is challenging to answer because most people fear what they do not know or understand. Fear can be a huge, negative motivation that elicits irrational behavior, even from the savviest parent. You can feel fear for your children in chat rooms, but you can also arm them to be safer in them.

Additionally, who really understands the Internet? Who really understands the chat rooms? More importantly, who really understands the child predators lurking behind keyboards anonymously in these online areas? Does anyone know where the predators lurk and how they use these chat rooms to trap kids?

DON'T GET PWNed!

Yes, we do. And so can you.

You can do a lot in the prevention arena for your children as they go in and out of chat rooms. Take the advantage over predators prowling for your children simply by increasing your knowledge of the Internet and taking charge of your children's online activities and habits.

Let's start with knowledge of what your children do and where they want to go online. First, there is a slight difference between instant messaging (IM) and chatting in a chat room.

INSTANT MESSAGING

While most think sending an instant message is an online conversation, it is only a conversation between two people. IMing is like email, but with an immediate response. And, just like email, it creates a direct online link between you and spammers, scammers, identity thieves, online predators, and cyberbullies.

8 INSTANT MESSAGING SAFEGUARDS

Teach your children to use the eight instant messaging safeguards when they instant message any of their friends. We've studied what's online and what the problems are and learned the ropes of instant messaging and can now offer you these safeguards. Teach your children to use them as if they were sending an email:

CHAPTER 4

INSTANT MESSAGING AND CHAT ROOMS ARE HERE TO STAY

- **IM Safeguard #1:** Choose a non-gender-specific screen name. Create one that does not directly relate to who you are.

- **IM Safeguard #2:** IM screen names, like email addresses, should be kept private.

- **IM Safeguard #3:** Never give out any personal information while using IM. This includes full name, telephone or cell phone numbers, address, place of business, etc.

- **IM Safeguard #4:** Never accept files or downloads from people you don't know.

- **IM Safeguard #5:** Know how to save copies of your IM conversations.

- **IM Safeguard #6:** IM only with contacts you recognize.

- **IM Safeguard #7:** If your children use a shared computer, do not let them use the automatic login that comes as standard with most instant message programs.

- **IM Safeguard #8:** If they use your computer at work, your company may have the right to view your conversations, so don't let your children use your work computer for private IM conversations.

Finally, it's also important for your children to know that instant messages are transmitted as clear text, using insecure Internet protocols. What does this mean in plain English? It means IMs may not be filtered by firewalls or scanned for viruses. They can be security risks for your computer.

CHAT ROOMS

Everyone likes a good chat. While the impression is that only teenagers utilize chat rooms, all age groups use online chat rooms spanning many areas of interests: From grandparents to collectors and hobbyists, many diverse groups use online chat rooms today.

Online chat rooms are virtual places on the Internet where people can type messages that appear on other people's computers almost immediately. More than one or two people at a time can be in a chat room and can take part in a conversation. Some of the really popular chat rooms have many people jumping in on conversations.

Online chat rooms are fun. That's why they are so popular. They have some negative publicity, due to ill-mannered people who frequent them as well as lurking predators. It's reminiscent of hula hoops. Years ago, decades really, the hula hoop was popular. Despite its sexual, hip-gyrating moves, a hula hoop was downright fun to spin. It's the same today with chat rooms. People can link up instantly with a group of new "friends." They're a modern way to enjoy social interaction, and they are fun to participate in.

That being said, we realize that predators of the worst kind hang out where kids and teens are: online and in the chat rooms.[11] You also need to know they are trolling for and setting traps for you and your child. They are there disguised as chat room members and friends solely for the purpose of catching a victim. You can make sure that victim is not you or your child.

First, chat rooms have no privacy whatsoever. Anyone and everyone is privy to things discussed, shared, and typed in the chat room. For all we know, messages are bouncing off computers on Saturn and being eavesdropped on by beings on Pluto. The point here is, there is no privacy online, especially in chat rooms.

Discuss this fact with your children. Talk about it and help them understand that being in a chat room means being just a little more careful about what they say online and who they consider friends. Then, lead into some safety rules. Teach them about the dangers in chat rooms and how to avoid them. Education is the key. Educate your children about the realities of chat rooms and how to use them safely.

Chats are also anonymous because participants use usernames and nicknames to identify themselves. It is this anonymity that is also very attractive to criminals. How much easier can it be for them? It is the notorious sexual predators and the cyberbullying that brings the worst of the chat room use to the foreground. They are the problem, not the chat rooms themselves.

As a parent, set up rules for your children in chat rooms. Monitor their use. Sit with them when they are in it sometime. Learn the lingo. "Chat room speak" is a language all its own and is based on abbreviations. If your children are older, limit their time in chat rooms, and ask to monitor it as well.

8 CHAT ROOM SAFETY SECRETS

We've studied enough chat rooms online to understand the problems that go along with them. Teach your child to use these eight chat room safety secrets as a guide when they head into them to interact with cyber-friends:

- **Chat Room Safety Secret #1:** Never give out your personal information in a chat room.

- **Chat Room Safety Secret #2:** Never agree to meet a stranger in person whom you met in a chat room.

- **Chat Room Safety Secret #3:** When you're asked to enter or sign up for a chat nickname, choose a name that doesn't give away your personal information.

- **Chat Room Safety Secret #4:** Be wary of other chatters who ask you to meet in private chat rooms. A private chat room is a room set up by an individual that is accessible by invitation only. Usually, it's an email invite, and it's a good idea your children stay out of them.

- **Chat Room Safety Secret #5:** Check the terms and conditions, code of conduct, and privacy statement at the chat site before you begin chatting.

- **Chat Room Safety Secret #6:** Tell your children that if something in a chat room makes them feel uncomfortable, they should immediately leave the chat room and tell an adult.

- **Chat Room Safety Secret #7**: Insist that your children never send photographs of themselves to anyone they meet in a chat room.

- **Chat Room Safety Secret #8:** Have your children stick to moderated chats. A moderated chat room is one that has someone watching, or "policing," and keeping the content and users in line. They delete inappropriate content and users.

Finally, as your children frequent the chat rooms, spyware removal software is good to have on your computer. Cookies and other spyware are deposited on your computer, even by mistakenly visiting sites. Make sure you can remove them effectively.

THE FEDS ARE WATCHING

We've mentioned earlier that the real problem online are the predators and criminals and how they utilize the anonymity of the Web for their purposes. It's not the search engines or chat rooms that are the problem. They are simply the vehicles for the predators.

On the other hand, some of them, MySpace and Facebook in particular, have been singled out by the government because they have not done enough to protect the kids online or filter out and stop the predators. It's a valid complaint.

It's changed, however, since January, 2008. MySpace, "the place for friends," is now working hard to distance itself from being identified as a place for pedophiles and pornography. While we know dangers to children online lurk everywhere, new legislation in the U.S. targets MySpace in particular.

We think it will help. Here's what happened: On January 14, 2008, forty-nine Attorneys General signed a document under which

MySpace agrees to make several changes.

The changes are primarily for protecting the younger kids, the minors who are members. (It's fascinating to note that Texas held out because they did not think the new regulations went far enough or were tough enough—good 'ol Texas!) Some of the things MySpace has agreed to include:

- Improving software that identifies underage users.

- Allowing parents to send their child's email address to the site so MySpace can restrict the child from signing in.

- Creating a closed "high school" section that makes it harder for adults to contact children.

- Dedicating resources to educating children and parents about internet safety.[12]

There are additional things they will do that include preventing the site from harboring child pornography rings. This will occur by MySpace obtaining and constantly updating a list of pornographic Websites and regularly severing any links between them and MySpace. MySpace is also retaining a contractor to identify and eliminate inappropriate images.[13]

Did MySpace step up and do all this willingly? No, we don't think so. It strictly comes from the pressure of Federal prosecution. Several states have been seeking to sue MySpace using a lawsuit that attacked the tobacco industry for marketing a dangerous product to kids as precedent. While MySpace may have only relented under this threat, the changes for our kids are a positive thing. Who cares today why they are making the changes. Its great they are.

CHAPTER 4

INSTANT MESSAGING AND CHAT ROOMS ARE HERE TO STAY

For now, these changes are just for MySpace. Facebook has also been subpoenaed and, as of this writing, seems to be relenting. We all know these sites are not the only social networking playgrounds for predators. They are just the most visible.

These two sites are not any more dangerous than other social networking sites; they just get more publicity as they are the largest with their 100 million visitors. Be smart as a parent. Don't wait for every social network site to be subpoenaed before your child can be safer on the Internet. Your children can be safer online if you, the parent, are smart about teaching them the basics of online safety in chat rooms. If you're completely relying on others to safeguard you when you are on the Internet, you're endangering yourself, no matter what your age, and your child.

The old adage, "Better safe than sorry" is a good rule of thumb when on the Web, and, there are many ways to increase safety that are better than making more laws. No matter what states, officials, or sites such as MySpace do, the most important thing for you is parental guidelines for when your child is online.

CHAPTER SUMMARY

- Take the advantage away from predators prowling for your children simply by increasing your knowledge of the internet and taking charge of your children's online activities and habits.

- Instant messaging is simply a conversation between two people, like email, but in real time.

- The 8 Easy Chat Room Safety Secrets:

  √ **Chat Room Safety Secret #1:** Never give out your personal information in a chat room.

  √ **Chat Room Safety Secret #2:** Never agree to meet a stranger in person whom you met in a chat room.

  √ **Chat Room Safety Secret #3:** When you're asked to enter or sign up for a chat nickname, choose a name that doesn't give away your personal information.

  √ **Chat Room Safety Secret #4:** Be wary of other chatters who ask you to meet in private chat rooms.

  √ **Chat Room Safety Secret #5:** Check the terms and conditions, code of conduct, and privacy statement at the chat site before you begin chatting.

  √ **Chat Room Safety Secret #6:** Tell your children that if something in a chat room makes them feel uncomfortable, they should immediately leave the chat room and tell an adult.

  √ **Chat Room Safety Secret #7:** Insist that your children never send photographs of themselves to anyone they meet in a chat room.

√ **Chat Room Safety Secret #8:** Have your children stick to moderated chats.

- Spyware removal software is good to have on your computer.

CHAPTER 5
ONLINE SEXUAL PREDATORS

THE SLY DISGUISES OF ONLINE SEXUAL PREDATORS

As mentioned earlier, it's the predators online that are the problem, not the search engines or the chat rooms. The predators use Websites as mechanisms to troll for our kids. It is important to focus on them as the real problem first. Therefore, the solution is in limiting their ability to snare victims.

A good first step for anyone is to take control of your own online safety. When you do that and learn some preventative techniques, you can then teach them to your child. Begin this process by understanding the diabolical ways predators prowl for kids. It will bring you one step closer to teaching your child to be safer. It also empowers you, the parent, to take action and not feel like a helpless victim.

With that, know that it is impossible to stop all the sexual predators online. Our approach is to arm you with our best information so you can stay one step ahead of these derelict individuals. It's about education and knowledge for better safety.

DON'T GET PWNed!

HOW TO PROTECT YOUR CHILD ONLINE

So, let's look at how the Internet is used by predators. You already know they use it to find victims. They can hide behind a layer of anonymity that offline sexual predators do not have. Anyone online can easily hide behind a username and password and prowl Websites and social networks with a free email account. They can be overt and announce they are adults or pretend to be other kids or teens. Predators can also pose as someone in a position of knowledge and power, such as a teacher or a coach.

Online predators also spend the majority of their time searching for kids and setting up traps and snares. It is a full-time passion spent as a full-time job as they hunt for victims. They use their time, creativity, and anonymity to troll for unsuspecting children in a number of ways.

Some predators like to befriend a child first. Often, this process involves lots of attention, kindness, and even gifts offered by the predator to the child. This type of predator is very, very patient and will take the time to allow the trap to develop. This process will also slowly introduce sexual context and content into conversations and communications with kids.

Some predators immediately engage in sexually explicit conversations with children. Teenagers are particularly targeted because of their natural curiosity about sex due to their developing sexual nature. Online sexual predators exploit this. Again, predators can pretend to be other teens, adding an element of deceit to the conversation.

Still other predators collect and trade child pornographic images. Many predators seek real face-to-face meetings with kids. Regard-

ONLINE SEXUAL PREDATORS

less of the approach, it is important to know that Dr. Fred Berlin, a leading researcher and an associate professor at the Johns Hopkins University School of Medicine, thinks it is impossible to identify sexual predators.[14] They can be any age or sex. There is no one type to filter out, catch, or prevent from prowling as they wish.

Second, the ease of access to the Internet attracts predators, too. Cars, gasoline, security cameras, and witnesses are just some of the things that predators eliminate in their stalking of victims online.

Now that you have an idea of how predators use the Internet for their sinister deeds, let's look at how you can begin to tell if your child is a victim of an online predator.

THE WARNING SIGNS

Just how can you tell if your child has been contacted by an online predator? If your child does not come and tell you, it's tough, no doubt about it. However, there are a few warning signs you can see that may indicate your child is caught in a trap. The following are some signs you can use that are a summation of what the FBI disseminates,[15] and they are great guidelines:

First, one of the most overt warning signs your child may be in the throes of being victimized online is that he may become withdrawn from the family. Online predators will work very hard at driving a wedge between children and their families. They do this is by accentuating any minor problems at home that your child might have.

HOW TO PROTECT YOUR CHILD ONLINE

The predator poses as an understanding friend, sometimes the only understanding friend, and can then drive a wedge into the family structure. This is not always the reason children withdraw, but it can be an indication of contact with online predators.

Another warning sign would be if your child displays anxious behavior about going to a particular place or seeing a particular person. Another indicator is your child may suddenly have behavior problems such as aggressiveness or extreme mood swings such as brooding, crying, or fearfulness. Her grades may also take a nosedive.

Your child may want to spend an excessive amount of time online rather than in other family activities or other offline social events. He may only want to be online when you are not around or overtly violate any online rules you, the parent, create.

Again, these are some potential warning signs. You have to take the initiative if any one of these is present. What is it exactly you need to do? Talk to your child. Ask her what is going on. If she won't talk to you, have her talk to another trusted adult. As an extreme measure, take away her online privileges because the bond between the predator and the child must be broken off immediately.

Do something; take action to get involved and cut off the contact with the predator. Contact by sexual predators and abuse online by them should first be reported to your local law enforcement in your town or area. There are some really great resources online that work in conjunction with law enforcement once the incident has gotten into the hands of the right officials. The best of the law enforcement sites, in our opinion, are:

CHAPTER 5

- **OnGuard Online: FTC Safety Tips**

  http://onguardonline.gov/socialnetworking.htrml

The government publishes a "Parent's Guide" to social networking. More importantly, they have a reporting mechanism for many types of problems encountered online.

- **Internet Crime Complaint Center**

  http://ic3.gov

IC3's mission is to serve as a vehicle to receive, develop, and refer criminal complaints regarding the rapidly expanding arena of cyber crime. The IC3 gives the victims of cyber crime a convenient and easy-to-use reporting mechanism that alerts authorities of suspected criminal or civil violations. There are also links to the FBI, National White Collar Crime Center, and the Bureau of Justice Assistance on the home page.

- **National Crime Prevention Council**

  http://ncpc.org

This government site has lots of information and resources for you on many crime prevention areas including cyber crime.

DON'T GET PWNed!

HOW TO PROTECT YOUR CHILD ONLINE

THE DANGERS OF SOCIAL NETWORKS AND BLOGS

We all have seen the headlines in the news. Predators have snared victims whom they met on social networks or blogs such as MySpace, Friendster, Xanga, and Facebook. We've grown accustomed to seeing generic headlines like these everyday:

"Myspace Predator Caught after Fleeing to South Carolina"

"Alarm over Facebook Predator"

"Girl, 13 Molested by MySpace Predator"

These sites are places where people can meet, communicate, and interact with each other online. They are very popular, and memberships are exploding in growth. Anyone who can get online can join and start interacting with each other immediately.

When they were invented, they were a brilliant idea. No one really understood at the time how predators would use them to snare victims. Now, there are stories daily about kids of all ages being caught in a predator's trap through a social network site.

First of all, these Websites are not going away. They represent substantial advertising dollars and billions in potential revenue to companies. CNN for example, reports the number of visitors to MySpace went from 4.9 million in 2005 to over 67 million in 2006. A report from October 2006 had it at 243 percent growth. Recent reports in 2007 show similar gains in visitors.[16]

It's not just MySpace. Social networking sites are popping up weekly, fueled by the speculation of their market value to advertisers. Ideas and excitement for such sites are expanding. There are now scrapbooking and photo sites such as Facebook that encourage innocent posting of family photos, including those of children.

Again, this is an example of another brilliant idea fraught with danger. Wherever there are children, even photos of children, predators hang out. Count on it.

We believe that most activity within these networks and blogs is legal and positive. The predators are the problem. The best way to insure safety for your children if they visit these sites is the knowledge we are arming you with and a few simple rules set up by you, Mom and Dad.

First, many kids are not aware they are putting themselves in danger by giving out too much personal information and communicating with people they've only met online. There are mainly two reasons for this. As we explained in chapter two, most kids today, especially teenagers, use the Internet as if it were a cell phone. On top of that, problems encountered online get larger because most kids, again, especially teenagers, do not inform their parents of online incidents. Let's look at these two important issues.

THE INTERNET IS NOT A CELL PHONE

Cell phones are the tip of the Internet iceberg. Mobile devices are becoming smaller, cheaper, and easier to use. This means easy access to the Internet anywhere, anytime, by anyone with one of these handheld wonders. Because they are so easy to use they work like a cell phone. It all adds up to encouraging carelessness in using them.

You can't blame the kids. Try to find a teenager today who does not have one. Nearly half of all kids ten to eighteen years old have one.[17] Mobile phone companies are targeting the new "12 and under" age group with their devices.[18]

Anyone using a cell phone is easily able to connect one-on-one with a friend. Chatting, "dissing" the student in English and screaming about their parent's overbearing rules is possible for any kid at any time. Without being overheard by another student lurking in the hallways or mom or dad in the kitchen, teenagers across the globe can talk friends and say anything they want via their cell phones. The unfortunate thing is that kids apply how they use their cell phones to how they use the Web and go online.

First, anything done on the Internet is NEVER a one-on-one conversation with anyone. The real danger here is that kids today have no idea this is true. They get online in a chat room with someone and let loose with all the personal information just as if they were on a cell phone, one-on-one with a friend.

Nothing could be further from the truth. Nothing could be more dangerous.

No one is ever alone online. This also means no one is ever alone in a chat room or on a social network site. And, even if they ever managed to make the impossible happen and be alone, anything and everything online can resurface or be found, traced, and saved by anyone at anytime. Once more, the Internet is not a cell phone. It should never be used as one, either.

I DON'T WANT TO TELL MY PARENTS

Many teenagers do not feel comfortable talking to their parents about personal things that happen to them. That's a shame. Kids, teens especially, need a "go to" person for those most intimate chats about feelings. It had better be Mom and Dad. If its not, they will seek someone out, and that someone may not necessarily be the best influence on them: gangs, peers, or inappropriate adults.

Sometimes, a child can seek out a good role model who will change their life. It happens. It could be a teacher, a coach, or close family friend. We're saying, don't leave this to chance. Make it be you, their parents, they seek out. When online incidents happen, especially contact from sexual predators, it is important that your child have help in dealing with them effectively. You need to provide that help. You will only know, however, that they are in trouble if they come and tell you.

Developing a relationship like this takes time. If your child grew up knowing that they could come to you, then continue to build on it. Set up rules and regulations for their time online, explain why, and then let them know they can and should come to you if anything uncomfortable happens.

If they do not have this type of relationship with you right now, start it. You and your teenager have a challenging road ahead of you, but it is never too late to start building trust and respect with them. They will need it to be safe online.

THE PREDATORS ARE NOT INTERESTED IN CHANGING OR BEING REHABILITATED

We're teaching you how to protect your child online. We're teaching you the basics of prevention. Why? It is harder to catch and change the predators. It is impossible to police the Internet. We can keep more people safe by teaching them to take charge of their lives and safety than by concentrating on catching and rehabilitating the criminals.

It is very difficult to rehabilitate child predators, especially sexual predators. It can be done, but the start of a change process like this must stem from the predator wanting to change. Many do not want to change. Many are not caught. Those that are caught and convicted have a 35 percent recidivism rate according to a study by the John Howard Society of Alberta in 1997.[19]

Take charge. Put the responsibility and the action in your hands. It's the best way to keep yourself and your child and family safe online.

CHAPTER SUMMARY

- The predators use the Internet as a mechanism to troll for our kids. Limiting their ability to prowl and snare victims is the foremost way to stop them.

- It is impossible to stop all the sexual predators online.

- Predators hide behind a layer of anonymity that offline sexual predators do not have.

- Online predators spend the majority of their time searching for kids and setting up traps and snares. It is a full-time passion spent as a full-time job as they hunt for victims.

- Some predators immediately engage in sexually explicit conversations with children.

- Other predators collect and trade child pornographic images. Many predators seek real face-to-face meetings with kids.

- There is no one profile for an online sexual predator. They can be any age or sex. There is no one type to filter out, catch, or prevent from prowling as they wish.

- The ease of access to the Internet attracts predators, too. Cars, gasoline, security cameras, and witnesses are just some of the things that predators eliminate in their stalking of victims online.

- The warning signs that your child may be caught in a trap by an online sexual predator are:

  √ They may become withdrawn from the family.

  √ Your child displays anxious behavior about going to a particular place or seeing a particular person.

√ Your child may suddenly have behavior problems such as aggressiveness or extreme mood swings such as brooding, crying, or fearfulness. School grades may take a nosedive without apparent reason.

√ Your child may want to spend an excessive amount of time online rather than in family activities or other offline social events.

√ Your child may only want to be online when you are not around or may overtly violate any online rules you, the parent, create.

- If any warning signs surface:

  √ Talk to your child.

  √ Ask them what is going on.

  √ Have them talk to a trusted adult if they won't talk to you.

  √ Take away their online privileges and break the bond created by the predator.

  √ Report any contact by sexual predators and abuse online to your local law enforcement.

- Many kids are not aware they are putting themselves in danger by giving out too much personal information and communicating with people they've only met online.

- The internet is not a cell phone. It should never be used as one, either.

- Kids, teens especially, need a "go to" person for those most intimate chats about feelings.

- When online incidents happen, especially contact from sexual predators, it is important that your child have help in dealing with them effectively.

- Take charge. Put the responsibility and the action in your hands. It's the best way to keep yourself and your child and family safe online.

CHAPTER 6

10 THINGS YOU CAN DO IMMEDIATELY TO KEEP YOUR CHILD SAFE ONLINE

WHERE REAL SAFETY BEGINS

Real online safety starts with the parents. It starts with Mom and Dad. Why would you, Mom and Dad, be the starting point of online safety? As parents you are role models, confidantes, and protectors of your children. You teach them what real love, respect, and trust feel like, so that they will not be mislead by the false version of these things. True safety online, true safety for your child in any situation, comes from you building confidence, trust, and respect. Yes, these are old ideas, but they still work today. A confident child is naturally less of a target for predators both online and offline. A confident child can make better choices when faced with a dangerous or threatening situation. Children who are guided through a learning process that demonstrates how to make good choices have solid, trusting, and respectful relationships with their parents. Children who have this type of relationship feel more secure and, in our experience, understand and execute the safety techniques we teach with more confidence and less fear of making mistakes. We call this the foundation of safety.

This foundation of safety includes online safety techniques, too. And parents, these are important because your children will be out and about in the world without you. They will be at the mall or online, and they had better know how to take care of themselves. They can do so when they have built confidence in themselves.

Confidence, trust, and respect are traits that take time to build. If your child already has them, you can increase their effectiveness with our techniques. If your child lacks them, you need to start building them immediately, no matter what their age. It is never too late.

Regardless of where you are at as a parent, continue to build the relationship with your child. While building it, incorporate these things you can do to keep your child safer online.

Print these out. Tape them to your computer. Get your child to do these things with you today.

THE 10 SECRETS TO STOPPING ONLINE PREDATORS COLD

Out of all we have studied and learned about the Internet and what can keep you and your child safer today, we've boiled it down to ten things. If you do any of these, or better yet, all of them, you can stay safer online:

CHAPTER 6

10 THINGS YOU CAN DO IMMEDIATELY

ONLINE SAFETY TIP #1:
TAKE CHARGE OF YOUR CHILD'S ONLINE SAFETY.

You're in charge, Mom and Dad. Real safety for your child begins at home. It begins with you. Feeling good and being confident, secure, and happy as a child is paramount to your child being safe. Take charge and let your child know you are.

ONLINE SAFETY TIP #2:
KNOW THE WEBSITES YOUR CHILD VISITS.

Monitor your children when they are online. Sit with them while they surf and play. If you do not sit with them while they are online, and your child is a preteen, consider installing available filters that let you control the sites they can visit.

It is not about mistrust, it's about knowledge. Preteens can accidentally visit a porn site where "cookies" are surreptitiously deposited on your computer. This typically opens the door for SPAM and more unwanted intrusions into your life.

ONLINE SAFETY TIP #3:
SET UP RULES FOR YOUR CHILD ONLINE.

Make rules you are comfortable with, and make them known to your child. We recommend setting a time of day your children can be online, limiting the time they spend online, setting guidelines for sites they can visit and ages of people they can communicate with. Set rules, make them known, and most importantly, stick to them.

DON'T GET PWNed!

HOW TO PROTECT YOUR CHILD ONLINE

ONLINE SAFETY TIP #4: TEACH YOUR CHILDREN NOT
TO GIVE OUT ANY PERSONAL INFORMATION ONLINE.

Teach your children to treat online contacts like the strangers they are. Personal information is none of their business! This includes telephone numbers, addresses, parents' work addresses, and names and location of schools.

ONLINE SAFETY TIP #5: MAKE AN AGREEMENT WITH YOUR
CHILDREN THAT THEY WILL TELL YOU ABOUT ANYTHING THEY
COME ACROSS ONLINE THAT MAKES THEM UNCOMFORTABLE.

This goes back to trust and listening skills and cannot be emphasized enough as important in your child's online safety. Kids need a "go to" person for those personal and profound confidential discussions. It had better be you, Mom or Dad. This stems from the trust and respect you build in your children as their parent. They will need you most if they come across danger online. Be there for them.

ONLINE SAFETY TIP #6: DO NOT ALLOW YOUR CHILDREN
TO AGREE TO MEET ANYONE IN PERSON THEY MET ONLINE.

It is never a good idea to allow your child to meet face-to-face with anyone they meet solely online. They reality is, that many kids are going to do it anyway. If they do, make sure you go with them and that the meeting takes place in a public place. Make sure you also view all correspondence that your child has shared with this individual prior to agreeing to this type of meeting.

CHAPTER 6

10 THINGS YOU CAN DO IMMEDIATELY

ONLINE SAFETY TIP #7: NEVER LET YOUR CHILDREN UPLOAD PICTURES OF THEMSELVES TO THE INTERNET.

There is no reason for a picture of your child to be posted on the Web without your permission. Digital photographs are one of the easiest items online to steal and abuse. If there really is a need for a photo of your child to be on the Internet, make sure you review the reasons why and carefully weigh the options. The best type of photo of a child to upload is a portrait with head shots only.

ONLINE SAFETY TIP #8: TEACH YOUR CHILD TO IGNORE ANY EMAIL, IM, OR CHAT ROOM MESSAGES THAT ARE MEAN IN CONTENT OR UNCOMFORTABLE TO READ.

Cyberbullying is a problem, as is sexually explicit material. Both have negative consequences for your child and need to be ignored and filtered.

ONLINE SAFETY TIP #9: NEVER ALLOW YOUR CHILDREN TO GIVE OUT THEIR PASSWORDS TO ANYONE.

Emphasize with your children that this means their best friends, too. Parents are the only ones who should know their child's passwords. Make sure you have them written down somewhere.

ONLINE SAFETY TIP #10: NEVER LET YOUR CHILDREN DOWNLOAD SOFTWARE WITHOUT YOUR PERMISSION.

Make sure nothing gets put onto your computer unless you know about it. This includes games, programs, and other materials that could include hidden items that jeopardize your family's privacy.

True online safety goes beyond this. The depth to which you can prepare your children for the dangers online, all dangers that they will face in their life, comes from building confidence, respect, trust, and integrity—true mentoring for a lifetime of safety.

CHAPTER SUMMARY

The 10 Secrets to Stopping Online Predators Cold!

- **Online Safety Tip #1:** Take charge of your child's online safety.

- **Online Safety Tip #2:** Know the Websites your child visits.

- **Online Safety Tip #3:** Set up rules for your child online.

- **Online Safety Tip #4:** Teach your child not to give out any personal information online.

- **Online Safety Tip #5:** Make an agreement with your children that they will tell you about anything they come across online that makes them uncomfortable.

- **Online Safety Tip #6:** Do not allow your children to agree to meet anyone in person they met online.

- **Online Safety Tip #7:** Never let your children upload pictures of themselves to the Internet.

- **Online Safety Tip #8:** Teach your child to ignore any email, IM, or chat room messages that are mean in content or uncomfortable to read.

- **Online Safety Tip #9:** Never allow your children to give out their password to anyone.

- **Online Safety Tip #10:** Never let your child download software without your Permission.

CHAPTER 7
YOUNG KIDS ONLINE

KIDS NEED PROTECTING

Parents do get it; their young children need protecting. Their children need the advantage of being around Mom and Dad wherever they go so that they can learn to cross the road, swim, and ride a bike safely. They also need to learn to keep a safe distance from strangers.

It's no different with online safety. Kids, especially younger kids, need protecting online. They need your protection, Mom and Dad, in person, right there with them.

TODDLERS AND PRESCHOOL

Toddlers and preschoolers online, you ask? Today, there are many educational sites and online development programs available for preschoolers. The good news is that they require a parent or educator to be online with them.

Going online with your toddler is purely a parental choice. Parents line up on either side of the "How young is too young" debate as vehemently as they support political candidates. Their devotion to their ideas of educating kids with online tools is as hot a topic as religion.

Regardless of where you are in the debate about preschool age online learning, we know two things. One, toddlers love to push buttons and play games. Two, there are parents who believe the computer is a great educational tool for their two-year-old.

The game-playing aspect makes a computer a natural for kids this age. Some parents believe they have found sites that entertain kids while also teaching them things. There are great places on the web that make learning the alphabet, numbers, colors, shapes, and music easy and fun. Therefore, we'll help parents who want to go online with their young child be a little more aware.

If you do take your toddler online, make sure you sit there with him every second he plays. Make sure you follow good online safety practices, even on sites with toddler games.

Never use the Internet games or sites as a babysitter while you cook dinner or focus on other things. In a few years, you will need to demonstrate that you are in charge of his online safety, and paying attention to everything he does online is a must.

Also, a toddler can disable, blank out, and mess up a computer in a flash. Be there to safeguard your computer. One wrong button and the "Geeks" will need to pay a house call. Last, but not least, a toddler on a computer is almost certainly sitting on a chair at a desk or table. This is a recipe for an accident for a squirming two-year-old if you take your eye off her. Many home accidents happen with toddlers falling

KIDS NEED PROTECTING

off chairs and hitting their heads on hard surfaces. The conclusion is, sit with your very young child while she is on the computer.

Finally, playing games with your child is one of the best ways, even at a young age, to build trust and confidence between the two of you. Play along with him. When he plays games, make every moment count as an opportunity to build a foundation for a lifetime of safety. Always sit with your toddler whenever you take him online.

ELEMENTARY AGE

Elementary age kids, those around seven years old, begin to be introduced to Websites not only from friends allowed online but through schools recommending educational games.

Many educational materials that were traditionally provided by textbooks are now loaded up on informational Websites. Some of these textbook-affiliated sites even come in game format. The bottom line here is whether you allow them to be online or not, your youngster will be surrounded by information, almost in the form of constant advertising, about the great things online.

If you do not allow them online, tell them why. "Because I said so!" just doesn't work anymore. When you tell them why, they may not agree with your reasons, but they will understand them. Honesty goes incredibly far when setting up rules and being a mentoring parent.

If you do allow them online, make sure a set of online rules and regulations are in place. Make sure you are educated in good online safety practices. For a child ages six to ten, make sure you actually sit and play on the Web with them.

When your child visits a Website, even a school-recommended site, make sure you know that Website inside and out. Sit with your child for at least thirty minutes and poke around and play on it with her. Understand where the links go and what information is provided on the site. If there are games available, play them. Screen out the site if there is any violent or excessively aggressive play in the games.

Check the pop-ups as they occur, even if it is time consuming for you. It will give you a good idea of the advertising allowed on the site. You'll want to make sure it is appropriate for your child.

Limit the time your elementary age children can be online. And, every time they are online, be in the vicinity of the computer, so you are aware of their demeanor and behavior while online. Limiting time online is also a good idea if you allow your child to play games. Their focus and intensity with the games and the virtual competitiveness can create a high level of anxiety in them. If you notice your child's behavior becoming too focused on a game to the point where they are short-tempered, irritable, and yelling, "Leave me alone!" it is time to pull the plug and get them back into real life. Too much game playing, in our opinion, compromises learning social skills at this age, not to mention the negative effects of the increased anxiety.

Whether they are dealing with gaming anxiety or an inappropriate website, children roughly six to ten years old need a parent teaching them the How Tos and the Whys of good Internet safety. Take the time to do so.

CHAPTER 7

KIDS NEED PROTECTING

ONLINE SAFETY PRINCIPLES THAT NEVER FAIL

There is no magic to online safety. If your children come across something that makes them feel uncomfortable, they need to know they can come to you, no matter what. Parents need to set themselves up as the "go to" person for their children. This means that your children feel comfortable coming to you to tell you about anything they need to talk about. This means you need to have good listening skills and a calm approach to things you do not want to hear or that are uncomfortable for you.

Many kids do not understand why things trigger reactions in their parents, just that they do. One wild reaction from Mom or Dad, and they will be very careful not to replicate that kind of outburst again. They will be very reticent about creating another similar situation. Fears, phobias, and behaviors are learned from parents. Children are not born with fears and phobias. They learn yours by watching you.

The one online safety principle that will never fail is this: your children need to feel comfortable and know they can come to you with anything they encounter online that makes them feel uncomfortable. It could be an email, a site they stumble onto, a photo they see, or an audio clip they hear. They need to see you calmly assess it and, if needed, take care of it for them by deleting it or closing it down.

Screaming, yelling, panicking, or demanding, "where the heck did you get this?" will do more damage than any Website they stumble upon their entire life.

The final thing to do with your child visiting a lot of online game sites is to have a good spyware removal program installed on your computer. The "cookies" deposited by these and other Websites will need to be cleaned and controlled by you on a regular basis.

CHAPTER SUMMARY

- Young children online need protecting by their parents.

- Allowing your toddler online is purely a parental choice.

- If you do take your toddler online, sit there with her every second she plays.

- Make sure you follow good online safety practices, even on sites with toddler games.

- Never use the Internet games or sites as a babysitter while you cook dinner or focus on other things.

- Playing games with your child is one of the best ways, even at a young age, to build trust and confidence.

- Elementary age kids, those around seven years old, begin to be introduced to Websites not only from friends already allowed online, but through schools recommending educational games.

- If you do not allow your children online, tell them why.

- If you do allow them online, make sure a set of online rules and regulations are in place.

- When your child visits a Website, make sure you know that Website inside and out. Check the pop-ups, as they will give you a good idea of the advertising allowed on the site.

- Limit the time your elementary age child can be online.

- If your children come across something that makes them feel uncomfortable, they need to feel they can come to you, no matter what.

- Parents need to set themselves up as the "go to" person for their children. This means that your children feel comfortable coming to you to tell you about anything. This means you need to have good listening skills and a calm approach to things you do not want to hear or are uncomfortable with.

- Have a good spyware removal program installed on your computer.

CHAPTER 8
TEENS ONLINE

"HE WANTS TO GO BY HIMSELF!" AND OTHER PARENT NIGHTMARES

Teenagers. It is about the age when kids turn twelve to thirteen that we get most of our panic calls from parents. These calls go something like: "My daughter wants to ride her bike to school!" (Deep breath, then repeated louder) "By herself! How do I know she'll be OK?"

For most parents, the answers rarely quell the panic-laden questions. The truth is, if you have teenagers, most of your work as a parent is done. When teens begin to ask, then demand their independence, your role as a parent evolves into one of simply guiding and mentoring your teenager into making good choices for herself. That's it. If your teenager does not know how to ride her bike to and from school safely, then she, and you, are in big trouble.

At this age, your teenager had better be able to perceive situations as they develop around him and then navigate those situations with good choices that he can make on his own. This applies to everything, but especially to keeping himself safe. Making good choices for himself is about avoiding danger. It's about seeing it develop in the early stages and staying away from it. True safety will stem from his ability to make the right choices for himself when you are not around. This is true at the mall on Saturday. It matters for online safety, too.

How you keep your teenager safe online comes directly from how you approach parenting. It's that simple. There is no magic potion for safe teens online. For your teenager to stay safe online, she must have her own ability to make good choices for herself. "For herself," are words that we cannot emphasize enough.

Watching, spying, demanding answers, and setting up unreasonable rules may work in the short–term, but backfire in the long-term as an approach to online safety for your teen, or any teen. Your demands and rules are yours, not theirs. If they do not internalize and accept them, they will not follow them for very long. They need to buy into and understand what good safety practices mean, so they can be a part of the solution. They need to feel they are a respected partner with you as they mature into adults rather than little children being told what to do.

Second, they need their independence as teenagers. They should begin to get it, and it's how you give it that matters to them. For teens, it is all about trust. Do you trust them? It is all about respect. Do you respect their choices? Yes, they want independence, but they need to know that you, the parent, trust them and respect the choices they make. As they move out on their own in the world, they need to know you believe they can succeed and that they have your trust and respect. This is the guiding and mentoring part. You must guide them into good choices for themselves.

TEENS ONLINE

You may not agree with their choices, but you have to respect them. If they make a bad choice, and they will, show them what the right choice could have been. It's a skill and a challenge for parents. There are no right or wrong approaches in doing this, just what works for you.

Anyone with teenagers knows that they can tune parents out in nanoseconds. It's part of being a teenager. At the same time, you have to be able to talk to your teen, especially about online safety practices. So, listen to them first before you speak. Good listening skills, without judgment and wild emotions, go a long way. This is especially true if you are listening to things from your child that you don't like to hear.

Listen to your child's ideas about being online. By opening a discussion with your teenager about the dangers of the Internet, you can teach him how to watch out for those dangers. He will be able to recognize traps and areas he should not head into because he has engaged in safety discussions with you as a respected individual sharing common knowledge.

If teenagers understand that anything and everything they say is being bounced off satellites around the word, they will be more cautious. If they know about the disguises of predators, they will be more careful in what they say, who they meet online, and who they agree to meet in person if such a situation arises.

For parents today, the reality is, social networking sites are here to stay. They are popping up weekly, fueled by the speculation of their market value to advertisers. Advertisers are heavily targeting teens to go online if they are not already there. Once there, the same advertisers are heavily pressuring kids to not only stay there, but spend increased amounts of time there, too. Unless you live in a remote cave on a deserted island, your child will face these advertising messages daily. For most parents, your teenager will want to be online and in some type of chat room.

What will you do? How will you handle it? How will you react? You may not allow your teenager online, but tell her why you don't. We say, educate teenagers about the dangers as you tell them why they are not there, and they will be safer. It's the reasons behind your rules that will make a deeper impression on your teenager. Ignore this approach, and you are putting them at high risk that sometime in their lifetime, they will come across a danger online and not be prepared to handle it.

"YOU DON'T TRUST ME!" IS BUSTED

When you tell your child to stay out of Facebook, they will cry, "Why?! You don't trust me!" It's not about trust, it's about safety. For example, we live in California—earthquake country. Our teenagers need to tell us where they are going and to be available at regular check-in times via their cell phones. They also need to check in if their plans change, and they are heading to a new destination.

This is purely a safety issue. It has nothing to do with trust or lack of it. If the earth begins to shake, we need to know where our

TEENS ONLINE

kids are, so we can go get them and have them home safely with the rest of the family. The last earthquake that hit the Bay Area collapsed freeways and crushed utility lines while buildings burned. All family members need to be accounted for.

Online safety is the same way. Rules are there because so are the dangers. It's about safety, not lack of trust. Holding your teenager to certain rules for their online surfing is about safety, not lack of trust.

Take the time to discuss the realities of being on Facebook or MySpace with your children. Tell them about some of the actual incidents that have happened on those sites. Tell them about the predators and traps that are laid for them. Discuss how they can easily get caught in them. Education goes a very long way in a preventative approach to online safety.

Parents can discuss the realities of being online with their teenagers without creating fear or paranoia. Discussing online realities with your teen can get them to really understand why they have limits, why they have to be careful. More importantly, it will give them the reasons behind the rules and, for any smart child, get them to want to take the right online precautions themselves.

One of the best examples in this safety approach for teens is to teach them that anytime they are online, they are not alone or one-on-one with their friend. Most teens equate chatting online and sending emails to friends as a simple, private conversation between two people.

Explaining to a teenager that everything they see and do online bounces off satellites, electronic waves, and optic cables around the world gets their attention. Explaining how someone in Sydney online chatting with a friend down the block can be seen by someone in Milan, makes them stop, think, and understand the need to be a little more thoughtful when online.

Couple this example with one on how people can disguise their true identity behind a keyboard, computer screen, username, and password. Let your children know that the new friends they just met online may not really be who they say they are. It gets their attention. Most of all, they get it.

CHAPTER SUMMARY

- When teens begin to ask for, then demand, their independence, your role as a parent evolves into one of simply guiding and mentoring your teenagers into making good choices for themselves.

- Teenagers' true online safety will stem from their ability to make the right choices. There is no magic potion for safe teens online. Your teens must be able to make good choices for themselves.

- How you keep your teenager safe online comes from how you approach parenting.

- You may not agree with your teenager's choices, but you have to respect them.

- You may not allow your teenager online, but tell them why. Teach them to respect you and your beliefs, too.

- Rules for your teenager online are for their safety. It's not about trust, it's about safety.

CHAPTER 9
THE CHILLING REALITIES ONLINE

ARE YOU REALLY PREPARED OR FOOLING YOURSELF?

Now that you've gotten through the techniques in this book, the issue that really matters is, "What are you going to do about it?"

Will you teach your child some or all of these techniques? Will you be proactive, and will you and your child be safer online? It's all in your hands. Start today. Do it consistently, and have a regular family check in every so many months.

Are you also prepared to be online? If you have read this far, the answer should be "almost." Now its time to implement the strategies and techniques we have presented thus far. This is the real key: action. Make sure you and your child are really prepared every time you both go on-line. Take action and implement the safety devices we have shown you.

TOO MANY CASE STUDIES TOO SOON

Why? Why are we taking the time to mention the obvious?

Even if you are armed and prepared and ready, you can still be trapped by an online predator. They are inventing, creating, and setting traps we can't imagine. They are doing this daily. Good people are caught unaware all the time on the Web.

What are some ways to deal with the realities of online threats today? We've all seen or heard in the news of the more sensational stories. We're all aware of the NBC show, "To Catch A Predator."

While most news stories about online predators deliver a dark side, they do have a somewhat buried positive contribution. The fear and paranoia these stories create motivate many into joining forces in stopping the predators dead in their tracks. They do bring to the fore an awareness of the dangers we need to be prepared for online. Perhaps the true positives in the negative stories are the lessons we can learn from them.

Those caught in the traps are the true victims. It's too easy in hindsight to analyze and dismiss the victim's actions as "ridiculous" when they get caught by an online predator. However, an awareness of just how trusting many people are online, how unprotected the children are, and how easy it is to get caught in a trap can help you understand just how careful you need to be, so you can stay out of the grasp of online predators.

Here are just a few of the stories out there. For each one of these, there are hundreds more like them. With a good awareness of what is

THE CHILLING REALITIES ONLINE

really happening, you can prevent your family from being one of the next victims. As you read each one of these, ask yourself how you would handle a similar situation. Ask yourself very carefully if you think your child could be caught in one of these, today, right now.

We're also not picking on anyone or MySpace. We want to provide this information as a final wake-up call to parents. If you've read the book to this point, the question becomes, what are you doing today? Are you prepared? Is your child safe online?

CASE STUDIES

CASE STUDY #1

A high school teacher was arrested and charged with having sex with two of his students. The police report says he used the Website, MySpace to meet, arrange, and encourage the activity.

The teacher arrested was the worst kind of predator. He used the naturally trusted position of teacher to catch victims. He was a twenty-three-year-old man seeking out high school student victims and snared them on an Internet site popular among those students. He had been with the school system full-time for five months, but had worked there part-time as a substitute for four years.

The teacher also worked in the Exceptional Children's Program and was a coach in the women's basketball program. Police say he met his victims at school, then used the popular social networking Website to advance the relationship.

The teacher referred to himself as "Black James" for his online persona and uploaded many pictures of victims and potential victims on his Myspace page.[20]

ASSESSMENT

We can only hope that school districts do background checks on any and all of the teachers who work for them. We suspect, however unfortunate it is, that some cunning, deviant individuals will always slip through the cracks.

At the same time, we don't believe MySpace is a place for high school teenagers to be hanging out online. The early intentions of MySpace, when it first launched, were great. But it has evolved into an open arena that is better for the adults who want to be on it. In its current state, MySpace is not a place for anyone under eighteen years of age. While they are putting controls in place to catch and screen predators, the stories continue about people being stalked, trapped, and abused by predators invading MySpace.

PARENT'S QUIZ

- Do you know the Websites your child visits?
- Do you know what they do online?
- Do you limit the amount of time your child is allowed online each day?
- Does your child know how predators set traps online?

THE CHILLING REALITIES ONLINE

- If they are contacted by a predator on MySpace, would they come and tell you about it?

- Would your child know that engaging in sexually explicit conversations online is the first indicator the person on the other side of the keyboard is likely a predator?

CASE STUDY #2

An Australian man was arrested after authorities say he sexually abused a fourteen-year-old girl he had met over the social networking site MySpace.

The twenty-three-year-old man was charged with five counts of sexual abuse. Authorities say he had met with the girl twice after contacting her online and suggesting they meet in person. At their second meeting, authorities say the man sexually abused another teenage girl that accompanied her friend to meet him.[21]

ASSESSMENT

What on earth is a fourteen-year-old girl doing playing around MySpace? This entire scenario, including bringing a friend to a second meeting with the sexual predator, begs for common sense. The girls are lucky they are alive. At the same time, the parents need to actively place rules and discipline measures into place immediately for both teenagers. Common sense guidelines online for these two girls may not work, and so actively cutting off their online privileges may be in order. We also hope the families engage in some professional help as the behavior of both teenagers after the first encounter offline with the predator is highly suspect.

PARENT'S QUIZ

- Do you know the Websites your child visits?

- Does your child know that she is not to meet anyone in person she meets online?

- Does your child assume that the other people online are exactly who they say they are?

- Do they know that wherever they are, online predators are, too?

- Is your child on MySpace?

- If your child were contacted by a predator on MySpace, would he come and tell you about it?

CASE STUDY #3

A father of four befriended a thirteen-year-old girl over the Internet before attempting to meet her for sex. He is now in jail for six years. The man, described as being addicted to Internet porn, was placed on the Sex Offenders Register indefinitely and banned from working with children for life.

He was also barred from having unsupervised access to the Internet. He initially contacted the teenage victim through a chat room.

CHAPTER 9

THE CHILLING REALITIES ONLINE

He exchanged sexually explicit messages for over two months with the girl and arranged to meet her.

The thirteen-year-old girl told the predator she was sixteen. She became frightened and fled the arranged meeting when she saw the older man show up to meet her. She ran to a nearby shop, where her father was called to escort her home.

There were many online communications between the two prior to setting up a meeting. Officers arresting the man discovered thousands of child porn images including clips of children being abused. A total of 11,574 images were found on the computer hard drive with 14,896 on an external hard drive he also owned. More child porn was found on a media player, and he had also set up files of child porn that could be accessed by other people.[22]

ASSESSMENT

What is a thirteen-year-old girl doing on MySpace? What is going on in this young girl's life that spurs her on to claim she is sixteen and engage in sexually explicit conversations with online cyberfriends. Yes, the predator is to blame and is in jail for what we believe is not long enough. On the other hand, this young girl has something going on in her life that needs her parent's help and attention. Would she have behaved like this without being on MySpace? Who knows? On the other hand, online predators have it too easy catching victims, and that is where we have to stop them upfront, proactively, before they catch anyone in a trap.

HOW TO PROTECT YOUR CHILD ONLINE

PARENT'S QUIZ

- Do you know exactly where your child goes online and what he does there?

- Does you child know never to upload a picture of herself to the Web?

- Does your child know that he is not to meet anyone in person he met online?

- Does your child provide personal information online such as her real name, address, and where she goes to school?

- Do they know that wherever they are online, predators are, too?

- Do you know where your child is heading with his friends today?

CASE STUDY #4

A twelve-year-old girl says she was coerced and threatened into sending naked pictures of herself to a friend via the Internet. The girl's family, not the girl herself, reported the incident to authorities.

It turns out that a family member discovered one of the photograph's the girl took of herself and then questioned her about it. She admitted to being in a chat room. She said she was coerced online into going into another "private" chat room. The girl said she was threatened into sending naked photographs of herself to the person with whom she was talking, but does not know who she was talking to or who received the photographs.[23]

CHAPTER 9

THE CHILLING REALITIES ONLINE

ASSESSMENT

Were there any parental controls in place for this twelve-year-old girl online? It is not hard to coerce and intimidate a twelve-year-old into questionable behaviors. This, however, is an extreme. It is possible the girl got herself into trouble accidentally and went to extremes to get out, intimidated by the predators. We hope that most kids, if they get into trouble, know that they can go to a trusted adult to get help instead of engaging in behavior that gets them into deeper and deeper trouble.

PARENT'S QUIZ

- Is your child comfortable coming to you when she gets into trouble?

- How do you know?

- Who is your child's "go to" person?

- Does your child talk to you about anything uncomfortable he comes across online?

- Does your child know never to upload a picture of herself to the Web?

- Do they know that wherever they are online, predators are, too?

DON'T GET PWNed!

HOW TO PROTECT YOUR CHILD ONLINE

CASE STUDY #5

On the same day MySpace and the attorneys general for forty-nine states announced an agreement that will put more stringent controls in place on the popular Website for kids, a Tampa man met up face-to-face with two girls he had met there online. He sexually assaulted them. After one of the girls told her parents what happened, the police arrested the man while attempting a second meeting with the other girl.[24]

ASSESSMENT

These stories are repeating themselves. When is enough going to be enough of this same thing unfolding? The penalties for the predators need to get tougher. The kids online need to get smarter about the traps being set for them. If you or your child do not know the first thing about being safe online, then don't open that browser window again until you do.

PARENT'S QUIZ

- Is your child on MySpace?
- Do you know if your child visits chat rooms?
- Does you child know never to upload a picture of himself to the Web?
- Does your child provide personal information online such as her real name, address, and where she goes to school?

CHAPTER 9

THE CHILLING REALITIES ONLINE

- Do they know that wherever they are online, predators are, too?

- Does your child talk to you about anything uncomfortable he comes across online?

CHAPTER SUMMARY

- Nothing is funny about predators lurking around the Internet or MySpace trolling for victims. What would you do to protect your kids from online predators? What do you do to protect yourself when you go online yourself?

- Do you know the Websites your child visits?

- Do you know what your kids do online?

- How long are they allowed online each day?

- Do they know how predators set traps online?

- If they were contacted by a predator on MySpace, would they come and tell you about it?

- Does your child know she they are not to meet anyone in person she met online?

- Does your child assume that the other people online are exactly who they say they are?

- Do they know that wherever they are online, predators are, too?

- Does your child know not to upload a picture of himself to the Web?

- Does your child provide personal information online such as her real name, address, and where she goes to school?

- Do you know where your child is heading with his friends today?

- Do you know if your child visits chat rooms?

- Does your child talk to you about anything uncomfortable she comes across online?

CHAPTER 10
PARENTING SECRETS FOR KIDS ONLINE

OWNING THE POWER TO KEEP YOUR CHILD SAFE

You can actually take online safety principles and expand them into larger arenas, like offline safety, too. Now that you know how to teach your child to be safer online, you can build on the information, tips, and techniques. How do we know? These are lessons we have learned from thirty years of teaching. Parenting is an integral part of safety for any child, anywhere.

The larger arena is for you, the parent, to develop your parenting skills so that you can mentor a more confident, safer child no matter where they are or what they are doing. More importantly, they can then keep themselves safe, no matter where they are, when you are not around.

Step one is knowing that your child's safety, whether online or offline, depends on you! There is no magic pill or quick fix or Hollywood movie to roll in front of your children that will keep them safer. It all is up to you, the parent, and what you teach them. It also matters how you teach them.

Safer children online will be able to apply what they know to also be safer offline. Why? Because you have taught them to make good choices for themselves, have enough confidence in their decisions, and to know when something that feels bad is to be avoided. We're going to show you a few tips for how to use the online safety information in this book to achieve greater overall safety for your child.

We teach kids to keep themselves safe. We also teach kids to be responsible for themselves. The most important thing, however, the crucial piece in making it work, is you, the parent, taking the responsibility for insuring it is all put into place. You must own the responsibility for keeping your child safe. You must make sure your children learn how to keep themselves safe from both offline and online threats when you are not around. It's all about them out in the world on their own, without you.

And, Mom and Dad, it is your responsibility to make sure they have this "keep themselves safe" ability. Easily said by glib safety experts, but what does this really mean? More importantly, how do you do this from a simple little book?

To be honest, it is pretty simple. It means you must stand up and grab hold of an incredible power waiting for you to command and control. It is called the "Power to Keep Your Child Safe."

Sometimes we call it mentoring.

Mentoring your child goes beyond parenting. It gets into making a positive difference by influencing your children to be the best they can be as individuals. Mentoring means you maximize your commitment. It means doing what needs to be done. It means when you're tired, sick, or fed up with things, you still take the time and patience to insure your children are safe for their entire lifetime. Being responsible means teaching your child to be safe in a constant and consistent series of small steps everyday.

Is it easy to do? That depends on you. What is your commitment to your child? What is your commitment to your child's safety? If you answered with a resounding, "100 percent!" then it will be easy for you. You're reading this book because you are already a mentor to your child. Your child's safety for an entire lifetime can be simple and easy added to the mentoring skills you already possess with a few additional safety tips.

If you have not gone beyond basic parenting, then we'll help you make the jump into true mentoring. It is one thing to understand responsibility. It is another to own it. Owning it is harnessing its power. Simply put, you own your child's safety. You make it work. Guide your child every step of the way in what to do and how to do it. Own the responsibility of making sure they understand how to keep themselves safe and learn it. Help them learn for a lifetime how to keep themselves safe from sexual predators when you are not around.

THE WORD THAT WORKS MIRACLES

"Commitment" is a word that, as an adult, you no doubt have seen and heard throughout your lifetime. It is overused. We hear it too much and can easily tune it out.

Be careful!

"Commitment" is a very powerful word that can work miracles. It is only overused by those who choose to ignore it. You should pay attention to this word and its meaning, especially when it comes to your child's safety.

If you worry about online predators, now is the time to pay attention to this word "commitment" with new interest and resolve. Few things are as powerful to you as commitment. Commitment can miraculously turn ordinary, sometimes less than ordinary, individuals into leaders, dream achievers, and successful human beings.

You must commit to your children's online safety. We have to ask: "As a parent, are you truly committed to your children's online safety?" Of course, everyone reading this book will say, "Yes!" But there is a follow-up question, and that is: "How much time will you spend each day carrying out the techniques and exercises we have explained in this book, with your child?"

Your answer to this question is a measure of your commitment. Time is a precious commodity for anyone, especially a parent, in today's fast-paced world. Time, however, is required for commitment. There is no way around it.

The online safety techniques and suggestions we provide take five to ten minutes to teach. Period. They take a few minutes a week, if that, to reinforce. A twice a month chat about goings-on online takes thirty minutes flat. That's all. Are you committed to that? How important is your child's online safety from predators? It is actually easier than that. If you understand what we are saying, if you embrace our philosophy of child safety, then the techniques are integrated into what you are already doing as a committed parent, not adding any more time a day to your already crazy schedule.

In the worst case, if the safety techniques added thirty or sixty minutes a day to your busy schedule, would your commitment still be there? Again, what price is your child's safety from online predators?

We are just making a point, here. We have intentionally made the information in this book readily available to you and easy to follow and use in minutes a day. You just need to commit to use it.

We hope your commitment is a resounding "Yes!" to your child's safety. Our methods do not require hours a day or even thirty minutes a day. However, the commitment is still required. "Required" is a harsh word when preceded by the word "commitment." We have a saying with the kids in our classes, "Too bad, so sad!" and we'll use it here. Five minutes a day or fifteen minutes every other day is reasonable for your child's lifelong safety. As a parent, you must be accountable for providing the impetus and commitment to achieving true safety for your children. We just make it simpler for you.

Committing to your child's safety needs to be viewed as a sacred vow. We are challenging you now to read every word of this book. We are challenging you to follow through on just 10 percent of what you read here. Can you do it?

DON'T GET PWNed!

HOW TO PROTECT YOUR CHILD ONLINE

View your commitment as the foundation of a lifetime of safety for your child. With a solid commitment from you, your children will see how serious you are about their safety. They will then take it more seriously themselves. It's called leading by example—another important step in committing to your child's safety. If you do, you will help your children be safe from sexual predators and be safer in all areas today then they were yesterday.

THE AMAZING POWER OF CLARITY

What will commitment do for you as a parent? What will it do for your child's online safety? The answer is simple: it will give you the power of clarity. It will give you a targeted purpose to focus on and a goal to head toward. You can move forward with the laser focused purpose of keeping your child safe from sexual predators.

Clarity allows you to filter through the maze of everything constantly being thrown at you and zero in on the things that are truly important for your children, such as their safety.

Clarity of your goal for safety will come with making a commitment to your child's online safety program. The importance of this goes beyond the obvious safety benefits for your child. Clarity benefits you directly, especially when you are struggling to maintain your commitment.

We all go through ups and downs in life. What distinguishes one individual from another, however, is strong commitment to a clear

PARENTING SECRETS FOR KIDS ONLINE

purpose, a goal. It is called goal setting. Commitment. Clarity. Goals. They all go together. Committing to your child's safety is pretty easy. So is getting started with it. Maintaining it can be a trick. Being human, we all go through times when our resolve may weaken. Find ways to strengthen your resolve.

For example, if your commitment to your child's online safety waivers, reread this book. Read other inspirational books. Talk to other like-minded parents about their commitment to their children. Find positive motivation in CDs you can pop into your stereo or your car. The solutions are endless, but keep your commitment to keeping sexual predators at bay and your child safe every day.

Also, keep your approach simple—the simpler the better. Clarity comes with simplicity. Keep your approach to your child's safety simple and easy for your lifestyle. When you struggle with your time, when it seems like your kids are endlessly crabby, when it seems like you just want to give up, the best thing to do to keep your commitment alive is reduce everything to its simplest form. Go back to the basics. Make everything simple. Refresh yourself. And, most of all persevere.

We are here for you. We work with families and parents, too. If you are truly committed to your child's safety, then you are truly ready to learn and implement real safety techniques starting with our 5 Secrets of Safe Kids.

DON'T GET PWNed!

HOW TO PROTECT YOUR CHILD ONLINE

THE 5 SECRETS OF SAFE KIDS

There are five secrets we have learned that truly make kids safe. These secrets set the foundation of true safety for a lifetime in children, online or offline, and can do the same for your children. These "secrets" will also surprise you. They work quietly and effectively on a subconscious level. If you use them, they will make any safety technique that much more effective. Without them, your children will never be able to keep themselves safe. Ever.

SECRET #1: CONFIDENCE

Confidence and a positive self-image are crucial in child safety. Confident kids are less of a target for sexual predators. Not only do they stand taller and keep their heads higher (the benefits of which we'll explain later), they represent a problem, a less than easy victim for sexual predators.

Confident kids project "struggle" for any predator trolling for kids, and more often than not, predators will pass them by. More often, predators, both online and offline, will choose kids who appear weak or sad, children in need of a friend. Online predators will use this ploy to begin to develop a foundation of friendship and trust with the child. Offline, these are the kids that hang their heads, shuffle down the street, and have a hard time looking anyone in the eye when they talk to them.

Confidence is a powerful deterrent. And yet, there is something more, something deeper when your child is confident. We notice

CHAPTER 10

PARENTING SECRETS FOR KIDS ONLINE

confident kids display certain structural changes, physical changes in their bodies that serve them better than kids who have poor self-images. Confident kids can control their physical movements a little bit better. At the same time, they can move more quickly and with finer control of those movements. We find confident kids can actually focus better mentally and for longer periods of time.

We've noticed this nearly every time we start a new session of classes. One boy we taught, Raymond, is an example. He was a seven-year-old boy whose mother enrolled him in one of our ten week sessions. He constantly looked at his feet whenever we tried to interact or chat with him. He hung his head, hunched his shoulders, and rocked from foot to foot during every conversation. "He doesn't have any friends at school," a small girl in class offered.

He was slow to respond to verbal requests. It took several commands and excessive encouragement to get him to physically respond to any challenge put in front of him. He was somewhat overweight and moved slowly, with a shambling gate. It took five weeks of constant attention and praise like, "Hey! Raymond! Glad you're here!" That was super! You're great for doing that!" "Raymond! Wow! You did that well! Good for you! High five!" before we began to see some progress in him.

Slowly, ever so slowly, young Raymond began to respond. By the eighth week of the class, he was bubbling with excitement every time he showed up. He was animated and chatting with his peers before and during class, too. His posture started to straighten, and he would meet people's eyes, though still warily. By the time our classes ended, he was laughing and smiling, standing tall and engaging others with direct eye contact. His physical command of his body greatly improved, and he was able to move more quickly and with greater control.

Raymond is not the only child we have observed going through these changes during the course of our classes. We have noted it time and again, class after class, year after year. It is a result of higher self-esteem and greater confidence that the child, in this case Raymond, experienced.

Confident kids are better equipped physically, mentally, and emotionally to learn the actual safety techniques that could save them from sexual predators. Kids who hang their head, shuffle around, or are tired or ill, cannot move with as much control or speed or think as clearly as kids who are healthy and confident. A high degree of self-confidence and a positive self-image matter in child safety.

SECRET #2: EMPOWERMENT

Empowering your children to take care of themselves is one of the most powerful safety secrets we can offer you. When you empower your children, you mentor them into making good, positive choices for themselves on their own. When they can do this, they will truly be safe for a lifetime.

In its simplest form, empowerment means your children feel like they have a measure of control over their life. They feel they can make their own decisions. Most kids don't feel this ability. Most kids

CHAPTER 10

do not have it, either. Parents and adults are constantly making decisions for children including:

- When to eat
- What to eat
- When to get up
- When to go to sleep
- Where to go
- Who to go with
- What to do

The list can go on endlessly. Life for children can feel completely out of their control. Kids will engage in a struggle with their parents to get some control of their lives. In doing so it usually comes across as conflict.

- No! I don't want to go!
- I don't like that!
- I'm not eating that!
- Stop it!
- I don't want to!
- Leave me alone!

The secret to empowering your children, even at the youngest of ages, is in giving them their own choices to make. Give them alternatives to situations in their lives; let them make some of their own decisions.

This too, can be pretty simple. For example, instead of telling them what days they can be online, ask them to choose between Mondays, Wednesdays, and Fridays or Tuesdays, Thursdays, and Saturdays. Offer them an option, a choice to make, instead of just telling them when they can be online. Another opportunity to give them a choice arises when choosing whether to go online in the morning, afternoon, or evening. You can also let them choose between being online an hour or an hour and a half at a time.

These same techniques can work offline as well. Instead of the picking the green dress yourself, ask your daughter which dress she would like to wear. Instead of forcing your son into the brown shoes, ask him which ones he would like to put on today.

These are pretty simple examples, but this is as easy as it gets when it comes to empowering your child. Giving your children choices is crucial to their development. It is also crucial to their ability to keep themselves safe.

Making choices matters to kids. When you do this simple, easy thing, miracles will happen within them. Empowered children start to feel good about themselves. And what would consistent, good feelings about themselves lead to? Confidence!

Will your child always make good choices for themselves? No. That is where you, Mom and Dad, come into the picture. You, as a mentor to your children, can guide them through the array of choices they will face. You can guide them and teach them about good choices and the benefits of making good choices for themselves. This is what safe kids are all about.

SECRET #3: CATCH THEM BEING GOOD

When your child makes a bad choice, it's important for you to stay calm about it. Yes, this is easier said then done. However, it is critical in your children's ability to keep themselves safe that you learn to take their mistakes in stride.

We want you to spend more time and energy catching your child being good. A subtle prodding towards better choices is more effective than highlighting, in a big, emotional way, any bad choice they make for themselves. If you have to highlight negative behavior, be very careful in saying, "That was a bad choice," rather than, "You are bad." Take care to say, "You can make better choices," instead of saying, "How stupid!" Things like, "You're a great kid, but that choice could have been better," keeps your child's image of themselves solid and highlights the choice only, not them, as being bad. Your child is good, the choice is bad.

Building confidence, building a solid self-image in your child, builds safety. Capitalize on this, and highlight the good things they do more often than the bad things. As a matter of fact, focus on highlighting as many good things as you can rather than making a big deal about the bad things they may do. Catch them being good.

We think positive reinforcement is a much stronger teaching tool and technique for child safety than negative reinforcement. Praise your children when you see them doing good behaviors. Lavish them with praise and adulation when they do really great things.

This is also positive mentoring. This is guiding your children into learning how to make good, solid, and positive choices for themselves. It builds and fosters that ever-so-critical confidence in them.

It is easier to notice the bad behavior. We are trained by society to notice the negative things people do. It is very easy to notice the bad things your child does. It is a focus of many parents, naturally. Reverse the trend, and make your focal point the things your child does well. If you praise your children every time they log off the computer at the agreed time, they will begin to repeat that behavior simply to get your praise. Positive reinforcement teaches your child to repeat those behaviors you want and makes it easier for you to guide them into those good choices.

SECRET #4: LISTENING

Another crucial secret to teaching kids to be safe is to let them know you are listening to them. Listening to your child goes beyond the standard, "Yep. Uh-huh. Sure." These kinds of responses, they get daily. True listening, the kind that allows your children to feel they are really being heard and understood, is a special parenting skill.

Listening to your children requires two things: one, you allow them to say what they need to say, in their words, in their way. It may be challenging to follow this advice, especially when your child speaks in disjointed sentences or jumbled words. They may take five or ten minutes out of your busy day, but just let them talk without interrupting them. You can tell when it is important versus when they are just mumbling or making noise. Sit and listen to them. Take the time to listen to your child, make the time.

Two, listen to what they say without judgment. Even if you do not like what you hear, even if you actually feel upset by what you hear, try not to respond negatively. Be quiet, look them in the eyes, and simply listen to them.

Your children come to you.. They need your attention. They believe at that moment you will listen to them. Do it. Reserve judgment and negative feelings about what they are saying for another time. When you do this, you are building on the future, on your children's safety. They need to feel, deep inside, that they can tell you about anything. They need the security of knowing you will listen to them no matter what. If your children are threatened in any way, online or offline, they will need to come to you, Mom or Dad, and tell you. That rapport needs to be established at a young age. You start by simply listening to them.

SECRET #5: REPETITION

This last secret is probably the most important of all. We can teach your kids in the classroom or provide them with valuable safety tips on our Website. We can put all of our information into a book for you to read. However, it is all useless unless you apply it day in and day out at home.

DON'T GET PWNed!

HOW TO PROTECT YOUR CHILD ONLINE

In our offline classrooms, we work with kids forty-five minutes at a time, once a week. You may read this book ten minutes a day until you finish it. True learning for your child comes with repetition. That is your job. You need to do it at home.

Repetition does not need to be boring, though. Make games out of the things you want to teach. Use fun words and phrases your child uses when talking about safety. Incorporate your children's favorite activities, toys, or cartoon characters into activities you do several times a week. It's repetition with excitement. What a great way for any child to learn!

Working with our techniques is also something to do a few times a week. Stay away from daily practice routines as if this were a sport, as this is the surest way to bore your children and lose their attention. Make learning about safety fun. Make it exciting. Incorporate the whole family, and enjoy learning about true safety for a lifetime together.

I WILL ALWAYS DO MY BEST!

We start our offline, ten-week safety program classes with the Keeping Kids Safe "two cardinal rules":

- I will always do my best!
- I will always say I can!

These rules are simple, yet they are highly effective contributors to your child's safety from sexual predators online and offline. First,

PARENTING SECRETS FOR KIDS ONLINE

we've mentioned that if your children are confident, they are less of a target for childhood predators. It goes even further than that. If your children can even create an appearance of being confident, happy, strong, and healthy when they are online, they can be less of target for online predators.

So what about the kids who are not so confident? This is where learning to appear confident can help. In our offline classes, we teach kids to pretend they are confident. What follows most of the time is that if we can teach children to pretend they are confident and practice this pretense, they will, over time, actually begin to evolve into confident children.

Offline, we teach kids to practice walking with their head held high, feeling good and feeling happy. When they do this, these fake feelings eventually sink in and take hold. We actually have a "Feel Good" game we play in our classrooms just for this purpose. Continuing to practice "feeling good" at home, with support from their parents, can really begin to set a foundation of confidence in most kids. They can even use this technique when online. Remember, when they are communicating feelings of being unhappy or angry, they are opening the door for predators.

We also use the two cardinal rules constantly, right from the start. Confidence in kids is so crucial to their safety that we use these rules all the time to build and build and build some more onto the foundation of safety we want to set in place. If we can get kids to recite these rules frequently, we can then begin to inject real feeling into how they say them. Pretending you're a confident kid is one thing, but adding feelings and emotion into it takes this to a whole other level.

DON'T GET PWNed!

KIDS AND HEROES

This next level we take it to is about kids becoming "heroes." Heroes are people who make a difference in other people's lives, thereby making a difference in their own. More than that, heroes are bigger than life to most kids: firefighters, police officers, martial arts instructors, soldiers, teachers, coaches, or even you, Mom and Dad. They are people whom kids not only look up to, but can readily relate to. Kids see heroes as being able to do anything. Kids want to do the same things, and therefore have a natural attraction to these people. We exploit this attraction.

We want kids to believe they can be heroes too. In our offline classes, we'll ask kids about their favorite heroes. As they often tell us, they know their heroes always triumph in the end. We simply tell kids that their heroes have special "powers," like confidence. We also tell them it is OK for them to have and use these powers, too.

It works.

We integrate this idea week in and week out into every class. As the class sequence progresses, we encourage the kids to stand up and tell everyone what they did that week to be like their hero. The kids look forward to this. At the end of each story, we applaud. The applause from the kids and crowd reinforces our positive, self-image building exercises. Approbation, acceptance, and encouragement enhance our effort to build confidence in each child.

When the children finish their stories, we seal it in their minds with, "That was super!" and "You're great for doing that!" These are very carefully chosen words. These words are about telling each child how great they are. We tell them the things they did were super, but they, themselves, are "great." It is just another building block in the foundation of solid self- confidence we want to instill in each child.

There is a series of hero games we play with the kids that again lead to developing confidence. One is called the "Feel Bad, Feel Good" game. First, we talk to the kids about how their hero always stands tall, shoulders back, head high, and appearing strong. Then we tell them we want them to look like their hero. They stand taller and stronger. We also tell them we want to play a game. Now we have their attention.

In this particular game, we let the kids walk around the room, and at the command of "Feel bad!" they hang their heads, shuffle around, and moan. We actually ask them to go back to a time in memory when they might have been sick or sad and remember what that felt like in their bodies. When they do so, we actually see some of the children sagging in their posture. Then we ask them to remember a time when they were really, really happy and excited. Perhaps it was their birthday. Perhaps it was Christmas Day, opening presents. Whatever it is, we take the kids there in their minds for a few seconds and here, too, we can see them physically change. This time, they straighten up as they envision their happy, exciting moments.

The start of the game includes our reminders of both of the feelings. At the command of, "Feel good, hero!" they stand upright, throw their shoulders back, hold their heads high, and smile as they stride around the room. At the command of, "Feel bad!" they slow down, slink and shuffle, and hang their heads.

Through a series of "Feel bad!" and "Feel good!" commands, we expose them to the way these two states feel. We want them to be able to differentiate between physically feeling good and feeling bad.

More importantly, when we see they understand the difference, we can then teach them to pretend they feel good even when they don't. What we are really doing is getting them to project confidence even though they may not feel that way at the moment, for any number of reasons. We can now get them to appear more confident all the time—especially when they are outside, alone, or online.

Kids can learn to fake out predators with these simple games by becoming less of a natural, first-impression target for predators. This gives children that extra edge of safety whenever they may find themselves without Mom or Dad. It's all about staying one step ahead of the sexual predators.

This same technique works for the kids online, too. When they began to feel bad because of something they have experienced online, they know they have to turn the conversation around to begin feeling good, even if they have to fake it. We teach kids online to never complain about how bad they feel or how upset they are with their parents in emails or messages because it draws the attention of predators.

We also find that if kids can begin to feel good when they need to or want to, they tend to like how it feels. They slowly begin to gravitate more and more to those good feelings we show them. It means they can really take hold of this ability, particularly if parents reinforce it at home.

CHAPTER 10

PARENTING SECRETS FOR KIDS ONLINE

The games we play merely introduce children to feelings of confidence. However, we find that kids want to build on them once they experience them. Playing games is simply the first step in an intentional sequence of safety techniques we want the kids to learn and embrace. It all comes down to our approach to safety, which is: teach kids to feel good about themselves; teach parents to reinforce this at home, and teach both the kids and the parents good, practical safety techniques.

THE HIDDEN POWERS OF A CHILD

Does it really work? Do kids really respond to someone telling them, "You can!" and "You're great!" and "Feel good!"? Do kids begin to believe in themselves when they constantly repeat, "I will always do my best!"?

We think so. Not only do we think so, we believe in it one hundred percent. We hear stories from parents that tell us it does work,.. A memorable example is from a mother who told us how her son was constantly the bench warmer on his baseball team. He was always the last one put into the game and the one ignored the most by the coach. The coach would actually tell her, "He just does not have much athletic ability at all."

At one point in the season, about halfway through a session of our offline classes, the boy "magically" began hitting the ball well, even scoring a series of homeruns. His batting became the best on the team, and his base running and fielding improved, too. When the Mother was asked by the coach how this "miracle" could have happened, the boy interrupted and chimed in, "Because Preston told me I could do anything!"

Is this a miracle? It depends on how you view things. It could be for you. We believe this boy began to realize his hidden abilities. We think the boy simply tapped into what every child has by nature, which is the power within them to do the best they can and be the best they can be. It just happens to be hidden in a great deal of kids through lack of belief in themselves.

Our society takes great care in taking young, wide-eyed, excited children and hammering them into compliant adults. There are societal benefits in doing this. We behave appropriately and strive to get along with everyone. We have laws and rules to follow that help keep the peace.

At the same time, most children slowly lose their dreams and self-confidence as they grow into adulthood. Doing so begins to bury those powers until they are deeply hidden. Who grows up wanting to struggle with money and finances and making ends meet? No one. Nobody wants these things, but they show up by slowly losing the understanding that we all have an inner strength and power.

Being the best you can be isn't really a mysterious power. It is a power and strength we believe everyone has, even the youngest children. We simply remind kids it is there. We simply bring out the power that kids usually hide under the surface. If they never understood before that they have it, we show them they do. If they already understand they have this great power within themselves, we show them how to build on it even more.

ONLINE PARENTING SKILLS FOR THE TWENTY-FIRST CENTURY

In teaching your child any of our online safety techniques, there is one essential thought to keep in the back of your mind at all times: keep it simple. If there is one parenting skill in today's busy, speed of light world that you must have, it is simplicity. Everything we do at Keeping Kids Safe is simple and executed with common sense. At the same time, everything we do is well thought out and based on years of experience. Most importantly, it is effective.

You will get better results, great results actually, when you keep your approach to your child's safety as simple as we do. Your parenting skills, while complex in nature, should be able to present the material in a simple, easy way so your kids can understand. The best parenting skill for the modern parent is simplicity. It is truly a twenty-first century skill.

A simple but effective way to begin teaching your child safety starts with a positive, fun, and exciting approach to the subject. Even a serious subject like safety and protection from sexual predators can be taught to kids in an exciting way with lots of positive reinforcement. We get great results with this approach in our offline classrooms.

So keep your learning sessions with your child fun. Keep them exciting. Keep what you work on with your child limited to short segments packed full of good feelings and laughter. Positive emotions are very powerful when linked to teaching and learning. When you develop parenting skills that can accomplish this, your child's learning will be accelerated.

You should guide your child through a path of learning online safety, rather than boring them with repetitive practice sessions and memorization. Good mentoring skills play naturally into reinforcing behaviors you want in your child, easily and effortlessly. It's true that what we teach in our offline classrooms is very powerful; however, it is still in a classroom. We are effective, but we still are an isolated occurrence once a week in the busy life of a child. Our techniques must be reinforced at home by parents for true, lifelong learning. Rote repetition should not have to happen, however, at least not with our techniques. Hone your skills, and make your child's path to safety easy, fun, and effective.

THE KEY TO PARENTING SUCCESS

"I will always do my best," becomes a lightning rod for growth only if it is incorporated into everyday life. This happens when it is part of family life. It happens when parents and entire families use and embrace the principles of safety we have presented in this book.

Growth and learning also happen at great rates in your children when you let your children express what they naturally possess. This is the key to success with your parenting skills—understanding your child's innate personality. The more you understand the core nature of your children, their basic personality, the more you can

PARENTING SECRETS FOR KIDS ONLINE

adjust your skills to play into their nature. You allow them to learn in an easier manner for them. You also reduce conflict that arises from misunderstanding your child. Just knowing the basics of your child's personality can help you teach them online safety in a more effective manner.

You can begin to do this with a simple understanding of the psychological make up of your child. First, kids are generally introverted or extroverted. Most kids are actually a mix of these two traits, somewhere between being introverted or extroverted. Psychologists have identified sixteen personality types indicating the various mixes of these two traits. If you are interested in an in-depth analysis, a licensed professional can administer a Myers-Briggs Type Indicator test. However, for our discussion, we keep it extremely simple with introverted and extroverted types of traits only.

Understanding which of these personalities your child tends toward allows you to guide her through life better. For example, if you deal with your introverted daughter as if she were an extrovert, you will make your interactions with her more difficult than they need to be. You'll be using skills that she either cannot respond to or responds to badly, perhaps increasing your frustration level. It can quickly spiral out of control.

An introvert is basically a shy person. An introverted person is usually characterized by concern primarily with his own thoughts and feelings. An extrovert is an outgoing, gregarious person. It is usually a person characterized by concern primarily with the physical and social environment.

HOW TO PROTECT YOUR CHILD ONLINE

It is crucial for you to understand that neither one of these personality traits is good or bad. They also do not mean that a child who is an introvert cannot develop skills in the extrovert arena or the other way around.

Most studies show introverts are a minority at around 30 percent of the population. If your child tends to be introverted, he may like quiet activities, especially ones he can do alone. Introverted kids are not antisocial, but they are exhausted by activities that most kids like, such as pep clubs, sports teams, and church activities.

Highlight and value the introverted qualities of concentration, focus, self-discipline, depth, integrity, and self-knowledge. Getting your introverted child's attention is pretty easy. Getting her to focus and increase her mental abilities is relatively easy. Teach her with an emphasis on her ability to work quietly and intensely alone. Help her allocate reading time and time to reflect on what you show her. At the same time, making her go out and play with all the other kids can be counter to her natural tendencies.

The majority of kids who run around, play games, join sports, and seem to run on boundless noise are extraverts. Our society values extroverted children highly. These are the kids who need high energy, excitement, and fun consistently built into their learning process. Play into their energy and excitement.

When you grasp the personality type of your child, you begin to increase your ability to guide him through life better. You can tool and tune your parenting skills to fit his extroversion or introversion. You can get results with your child in a manner that is more effective for your child and easier for both of you. You can guide him in positive directions more easily, and when you start to get results, you can increase your effectiveness and adjust your approach as required. More importantly, when you do not get the results you want, you can adjust your approach until you do.

THE AMAZING SKILL THAT WORKS MIRACLES

Our kids talk to us all the time. We listen, and we talk back to them. It occurs everyday, but how much of these conversations and interactions do you really understand? Are you really hearing what your children are saying from their perspective or are you interpreting their words from your adult way of thinking and perceiving? Learn to understand and interpret what your children are saying from their point of view. This is an invaluable parenting skill called "listening" and is at the center of any safety program for your child. You need to be able to decipher exactly what they are saying or trying to say when they come to you with an issue.

Good listening benefits you in many ways as a parent that go well beyond safety, including making life easier with less conflict for all involved in your family. It's what we call a secondary benefit of following our safety program. Good listening skills ease miscommunication and can eliminate a lot of misunderstandings that sap everyone's energy.

There are two keys to listening to your child effectively. One, learn to understand her words. How your child uses words and what your child means by them is very different from how you use those same words.

Start to create in your mind a dictionary of words your child uses. Understand and know her definition of terms and how she applies them at her age. Keep a watch as to how these definitions and uses change as she grows.

Two, take the time to stop, sit down, and look your child directly in the eyes when he has something important to tell you. This simple gesture subtly instills in your child the idea that you are there for him to go to any time he needs to do so. In terms of safety, he needs to know he can confidently go to you with anything. He needs to have a safe, secure feeling that you will listen to him.

Yes, every parent today is just too busy, but we are talking about five minutes of your time! What is your child's safety worth to you? Yes, your children come and interrupt you numerous times a day. You have the intuition, however, to know when it is really important. You know when you have to stop what you are doing, sit down, and listen to them. Take the time to do it.

Finally, whatever your child tells you, stay calm, listen intently, and do not interrupt. Especially if your child says something that is disconcerting, you must learn to listen calmly. The bottom line in safety is that you are teaching your child to come to you if ever she is approached or touched by a sexual predator.

You are showing your child that you, as her parent, are the trusted confidant she can go to, when anything uncomfortable happens to her, like being approached by a sexual predator online or offline. It is critical to her ability to keep herself safe that you become her "go to" person.

SECRETS TO DECIPHERING THE SILENCE

Your children also communicate in nonverbal ways. We all do. It's a great asset to be able to read your children's body language. It enhances your parenting skills and ability to teach them our safety techniques. This ability, coupled with understanding their personality traits and good listening skills, gives you a very powerful set of parenting skills. Again, the more skills you have, the better you can teach, mentor, and guide them in life and personal safety when you are not around.

Nonverbal communication is very complicated. However, there are some simple patterns and gestures you can recognize in your children that help you communicate better with them, especially when they are not so talkative. Observe their posture. Sometimes it will tell you more than their words. Keep in mind, these are generalities, but they will give you a basic understanding of what your children are really saying:

- Crossing arms and legs while standing is a defensive gesture.

- If they want to tell you they really don't like a person or what you may be saying, they narrow their eyes, tilt their head back and to the side, and keep their lips together. Folding arms always helps in communicating dislike.

- The main difference between sitting and standing is that sitting is a relatively defenseless position, almost forcing trust and empathy.

- Fibbing usually entails a lack of eye contact and excessive hand movements.

- Shifting from foot to foot shows worrying about getting found out. Also, it indicates that they want to go somewhere else to get away so that no guilty expressions are spotted like looking out the door, backing up towards the door, half-facing the person and half-facing the door, etc.

- Rubbing the back of the head can be a form of comforting oneself when saddened. It also shows impatience.

- Standing with arms crossed shows a sense of being 'closed'. It can also show anger, stubbornness, and assertiveness.

- Standing with one hand on the hip is the opposite of the above. It's suggestive of 'openness'.

- Inspecting fingernails indicates boredom or vanity.

- Hands clasped together or hands placed one over the other indicates deference and humility.[25]

What does this mean for you? It simply offers another communication tool for you to utilize in parenting your child and teaching him safety. Is your child bored when you are teaching him something? Spice up the excitement, or try it another time. Is your child angry with you? Chances are he is not going to pay much attention to any safety lessons for a while. Knowing these characteristics simply adds another element to your growing arsenal of parenting skills for better child safety.

POSITIVE REINFORCEMENT

It is so easy for parents to catch their kids doing the things they shouldn't be doing. It's too easy, for parents to highlight these negative things they see. Make an effort to highlight the good things your child does.

We teach safety to kids from a position of positive reinforcement and personal growth. We think we get better results with this approach. We catch kids being good and make it a point to praise them. Kids love praise. They especially love it when it comes from their parents. Your child lives for your approval. Approve of them. Be lavish with your praise. Do it consistently. Do it regularly. Do it with feeling.

THE NUCLEUS OF SAFETY

What does it mean when these skills of observing, listening, and giving positive reinforcement come together? It means a safer child.

DON'T GET PWNed!

HOW TO PROTECT YOUR CHILD ONLINE

These skills improve your children's learning of our safety techniques. They can be safe for a lifetime if you use them when you teach the actual techniques we will show you. Good parenting skills can make your child safer, and they benefit your family, too. Good safety and good families go hand-in-hand.

We call the blending of safe kids and good families, the "nucleus of safety." Maximizing its effectiveness depends on good parenting skills and commitment to being the best you can be, for both parents and kids.

Our nucleus of safety is for all families. We know that 65 percent of families in America today are headed by single parents. We know there are multi-racial adoptive families, foster families, and grandparents and aunts and uncles raising kids. The nucleus of safety is for all of you. It is for anyone raising kids or anyone who cares about kids.

This may seem eons away from stopping sexual predators, but it is not. Our approach to safety starts with us focusing on making stronger families. When we do that, we can also make safer kids.

So then, what really is this nucleus of safety? It involves family members coming together to stay one step ahead of sexual predators and stop them cold. It is our efforts and yours together that will make this world a little safer for every child. Five minutes a day means better kids, safer kids, better families.

CHAPTER SUMMARY

- Your child's safety from online predators depends on you!

- You must own the responsibility for keeping your child safe.

- You must make sure your children learn how to keep themselves safe from online predators when you are not around.

- Mentor your child. Make a positive difference by influencing your child to be the best she can be as an individual.

- You must commit to your child's online safety. View your commitment as the foundation of a lifetime of safety for your child.

- Clarity of focus and vision in teaching your child safety is powerful and will come with making a commitment to your child's safety program.

- Keep your approach simple. Clarity comes with simplicity.

- Learn the five secrets to keeping your child safe.

  √ Secret #1: Confidence

  √ Secret #2: Empowerment

  √ Secret #3: Catch them being good

  √ Secret #4: Listening

  √ Secret #5: Repetition

- Teach your child the two Keeping Kids Safe "cardinal rules."

  √ I will always do my best!

  √ I will always say I can!

- Teach your child to feel good and to be able to act confident even when they do not feel good.

- Remind your child often, "You can!"

- If there is one parenting skill to have today, it is simplicity.

- A simple but effective way to begin teaching your child safety starts with a positive, fun, and exciting approach to the subject.

- Keep your learning sessions with your child fun and exciting. Limit what you work on with your child to short segments packed full of good feelings and laughter.

- Understand which basic personality type your child is:

  √ Introverted

  √ Extroverted

- Most kids are a mix of these two traits, somewhere in between being introverted or extroverted.

- Understanding which of these personalities your child naturally is allows you to guide him through life better.

- Learn to understand and interpret what your child is saying.

- Listening is at the center of any safety program for your child.

- Learn to understand how your child uses words.

- Take the time to stop, sit down, and look your child directly in the eyes when she has something important to tell you.

- Learn to listen to your child calmly and quietly without interrupting.

- Learn to read your child's basic body language to understand what he is really saying.
- Catch your child being good and make it a point to praise her often.

CHAPTER 11
WHAT WORKS OFFLINE CAN WORK ONLINE TOO

ULTIMATE SAFETY IN YOUR NEIGHBORHOOD

The principles of responsibility, self-confidence, trust, and respect that enable children to keep themselves safe offline carry over to online safety. It carries over directly from life to the computer. The more you know, the more you can teach your child to be as safe as possible.

Total child safety—what Keeping Kids Safe is all about—warrants a few notes on how you can easily carry over safety for your child into any aspect of their life. More importantly, when they learn these ideas, they'll retain them for a lifetime of safety. As we say, "A safe child is a safe child is a safe child."

When your children leave your home, they are in the realm of offline, or direct, sexual predators. In your neighborhood, at your parks, on your streets, and outside the fences of your schools, direct sexual predators are surreptitiously hunting for children. You could choose to spend every second supervising your children from birth to high school, but how practical is that? How much trust and responsibility does that instill in your children? There is a better way.

These predators are hard to spot because they look like normal individuals. Your children can encounter threatening situations simply by playing in your yard while you are in the house. The best way to protect your children is to teach them how to keep themselves safe.

Step one is for your children to know how to effectively deal with strangers when approached them. Your children must be able to respond to, stay away from, and get out of developing dangerous situations. They must also be able to stay calm, focused, and apply any number of safety techniques if a situation rapidly gets out of control.

We have five secrets for playing outside that you can teach your children. They can use them immediately and be a little safer when you are not around. The secrets apply to any outdoor situation, including times when you are close, but not directly next to your child. We'll also show you how you can apply these five secrets to your child's online safety.

5 SECRETS FOR PLAYING OUTSIDE SAFELY

SECRET #1: TEACH YOUR CHILDREN TO PAY
ATTENTION TO THINGS THAT SEEM OUT OF PLACE.

Teach your children to be on the lookout for things that are out of the ordinary. Tell them it is OK for them to come tell you when they see something different. It does not matter what it is; just get them in the habit of telling you about things they see that don't seem normal to them.

Things out of the ordinary include people moving through your neighborhood who are not normally there, cars moving much more slowly up and down your street than usual, vehicles repeatedly driving up and down your street, or an unfamiliar service truck appearing out of nowhere one afternoon.

This same principle applies when your children are online. Teach them to pay attention to the tone of the conversation, the words that are being used, and the context in which they are framed.

SECRET #2: TEACH YOUR CHILDREN HOW TO SIT PROPERLY WHEN PLAYING.

Sitting properly means your children have their back straight, head high, and shoulders straight even when they are looking around or down. Show your children how to sit and play with their legs crossed and back straight. Sitting on their knees or with them bent to the side is also very effective for quick movement as long as their back is straight.

This sitting posture allows your children to spot things out of the ordinary and gives them an advantage if they need to stand up quickly.

Teach your children this new sitting posture with a series of really fun games. Call them silly titles like, "My Hero Sitting Game,"

"Who Can Sit the Longest Game," or even "I Can Sit Taller Than You Game." Whatever you call them, make them exciting for your children so you have and hold their attention.

Start by having them sit on the floor and remind them "Back straight!" and, "Head up!" Have them move around and do different things while on the floor. At random intervals, call out, "Power seat!" They must quickly move back into the starting position with their backs straight and heads up. Correct any slouching by repeating, "Back straight!" and, "Head up!"

Let the giggles roll as you play this game. Gently correct bad postures with positive words and guidance. Play the games with fifteen- to twenty-second sitting intervals at a time, then increase the intervals as your children learn to be more comfortable in this sitting posture. Be creative with the game and add your own ideas.

This is also a great game to play when your children are sitting at the computer. For health and physical safety reasons, your children should sit with both feet on the floor, back straight, and head up. The keyboard should be at a comfortable height with their palms resting lightly on a palm pad.

SECRET #3: TEACH YOUR CHILDREN
TO GET TO THEIR FEET QUICKLY.

In a potentially threatening situation, a child needs to be able to get up fast and move quickly, yet steadily. We teach kids to move fast, and we teach them to do it with control. It starts with being able to get up off the ground. With good focus skills, they can learn to do this easily and will be able to do it with a great deal of calm control.

The way most kids get up opens them up for being blindsided in an attack or abduction. Just watch your kids when they are watching TV. When they get up, they usually stick their bum in the air first, put their hands on the ground, and point their head down as they push themselves up with their arms. This method affords your children absolutely no protection or ability to see anything or anyone. Teach them how to stand up so they can keep their heads up and their eyes open. This means they stand up without bending over and without placing their hands on the ground. They can do this by raising up to their knees first with their head and shoulders straight, then placing a knee out at ninety degrees to their torso and rotating up and using the hips to reach a full standing position.

The end result is a child upright and alert and ready to move quickly if required. Again, teaching this technique to kids is done best with a fun game. Come up with a great name like, "The Stand in a Flash Game" and offer a reward at the end for your children when they succeed in moving in a flash.

Even better, you can tie this game to the "Sitting Game" in the prior secret. Have your children sit properly with backs straight and heads up, then have them jump up in a flash. The fun can really roll, and the learning can take hold when your children jump up fast, move around, then sit down quickly and correctly. Make sure each time you play this game, you offer a little more of a challenge, contest, or possible reward as they increase their skills.

Use this same strategy when your child is sitting at the computer. First, make sure they are always using a comfortable posture. Teach them to avoid hunching their shoulders and leaning over the edge of a desk. Then, teach them how to get up quickly and easily from the chair by swinging their legs to the side and standing up straight with their entire torso upright. Although it is not used often, we teach this to kids as a body-control technique. It teaches them to move from a sitting position quickly and efficiently. When they do that, they can easily apply the technique to a fire drill at school. If your child is very young, you can turn this exercise into a fun game. See how quickly she can move her chair back and stand up without knocking the chair over or injuring herself on the computer desk. It is all about children learning to control the quick movement of their body under all types of circumstances including physical threats. It leads to greater personal safety.

SECRET #4: TEACH YOUR CHILDREN TO LOOK PEOPLE, ESPECIALLY ADULTS, DIRECTLY IN THE EYES.

Very few children look adults right in the eyes when they are talking to them. It is an indication that they are intimidated by adults. Feeling intimidated by an adult is a child's way of showing respect to that adult.[26] Without destroying that respect, you can build self-confidence in your child by teaching them to look anyone in the eyes.

Looking someone in the eyes does many things for a child. One, it projects confidence that anyone approaching the child can see. Two, it allows the child some time to assess the intentions of the approaching individual. Three, a small child squarely and confidently looking at an approaching stranger in the eyes can give the child an extra split second advantage to flee a dangerous situation, especially if that stranger is surprised by the intense gaze of that child.

Obviously, your child cannot look anyone in the eye when she is online. However, the same principle of visual focus applies. Teach your child how to really see the words that she is sending and receiving. Help her to understand that certain words and phrases can be perceived in a variety of different ways.

SECRET #5: TEACH YOUR CHILDREN TO LISTEN TO THEIR INSTINCTS.

Another tool for your children's safety arsenal is for them to know that they have two brains, the one in their head and one in their belly. We call the one in the belly the "Belly Brain." Adults and teens know this as their "gut instinct."

Kids need to learn to listen to their Belly Brain. It is rarely, if ever, wrong. Kids have this gut feeling, too, but they need some help in learning how to listen to it and use it to keep them safe. Teach your children that the Belly Brain works for them. Teach them how to listen to it. Help your children distinguish between their Head Brain and their Belly Brain.

In our offline classes, we show the kids how their Head Brain can sometimes trick them. We use imagination and storytelling techniques that enable the children to build up a great, exciting tale about a shadow they saw dance across a wall. It's the same as when kids think monsters are in their bedroom closet or under the bed.

We show them how their Head Brain makes these stories up. We reinforce that the Belly Brain is the alarm clock for potentially dangerous situations. Teach your children to listen to and trust it at all times. You can show your kids how to recognize the uneasiness in their stomach without panic, alarm, or worry. When kids tune into their Belly Brain, they are better able to detect uncomfortable situations, questionable adults, and inappropriate behavior.

Kids naturally feel uncomfortable when they are around inappropriate behaviors or when asked inappropriate questions. We simply show them how to be alert to it with their Belly Brain.

When your child is sitting at the computer and he comes across something that makes him feel uneasy, or he is in a conversation that suddenly causes his Belly Brain to engage, he should immediately stop what he is doing and share that information with you.

ONLINE SECURITY IN NEIGHBORHOOD SAFETY CLUBS

Our goal is to help you thwart sexual predators that prowl your neighborhood and your computer. One way is to share information with your neighbors about any unusual or inappropriate situations that you or your child has come across, whether in your neighborhood or on your computer. If you are familiar with or come across new reporting agencies, share that information with your neighbors.

CHAPTER 11

WHAT WORKS OFFLINE CAN WORK ONLINE TOO

Some of our Keeping Kids Safe families have set up their own neighborhood safety clubs just for this purpose.

If your child is home alone and becomes uncomfortable with a situation that has come up on the computer or in your neighborhood, she should have an alternate safe haven she can go to besides you so she can share that information with a trusted adult. Give your children more than one safe haven in the event that one should be unavailable.

Set up procedures to alert you if they wind up in their alternate place. Whether you live in an apartment, condominium, or neighborhood with single family homes, it's a great idea to have a back-up safety plan with a second safe haven, so set up a safety option with your child as soon as possible. Walk them through the alternate areas and choices. Show them who to seek out and what to do once they get there. Set up your own neighborhood safety club to help your neighborhood's children feel safe and secure at all times.

CHAPTER SUMMARY

- Teach your child how to deal with strangers effectively when approached by one.

- Your child must be able to stay away from dangerous situations and respond to and get out of them if caught in one.

- They must also be able to stay calm, focused, and ready to apply any number of safety techniques if a situation rapidly gets out of control.

- We have five secrets for playing outside or on the computer that you can teach your child:

  - √ Secret #1: Teach your child to pay attention to things that seem out of place.

  - √ Secret #2: Teach your child how to sit properly when playing on the computer.

  - √ Secret #3: Teach your child to get to her feet quickly.

  - √ Secret #4: Teach your child to look people, especially adults, directly in the eyes.

  - √ Secret #5: Teach your child to listen to their instincts.

- Give your children more than one safe haven if they are home alone and come across an uncomfortable situation in your neighborhood or while on the computer.

- Set up procedures to alert you if they wind up in their alternate place.

CHAPTER 12

TOTAL SAFETY

THE AMAZING SECRETS TO KEEPING KIDS SAFE ANYWHERE

We are child safety experts. Why listen to us about any kind of safety, online or not? Simply because we have over thirty years of experience in doing this. We've created, observed, researched, and worked our way through this to find real, effective safety policies in the twenty-first century.

We'll prove it. We want to give you a complete picture of our offline Keeping Kids Safe program and how you can apply it to online safety for your child. There are a lot of ideas and safety techniques presented in this book. Now we will show you how we use it ourselves, step by step, in one our ten-week classroom training course for elementary age children.

Since our program is about kids and their ability to keep themselves safe, our focus is on each child who comes through the door of our classroom. From the time they step through the front door, we call all the children heroes. We use this tag over ten weeks with great emphasis.

It is a teaching tool, and it helps us get the results we need.

Why?

As we said earlier, heroes, for both boys and girls, are still fun and exciting. Fun gets kids attention. Heroes are real characters that are bigger than life. Whether it is a firefighter, police officer, doctor, martial arts instructor or you, the parent, these figures perform phenomenal feats that kids can relate to and understand. This analogy is the key to having the kids in our classes believe they can do everything we teach them. We continue building on those special hero traits each week. Without the kids knowing it, we are quietly arming them with a personal safety arsenal of techniques. Then, in the final weeks, we pull it all together for the kids and their parents with comprehensive exercises and play acting. We call them Hero Games.

So, what do we teach the kids, and how does this work? We teach the kids to move fast, and we teach them to do it with control. In a potentially threatening situation, a child needs to be able to move quickly, yet steadily.

We also show them how to "Sit Like a Hero." This means the kids sit down with legs crossed, hands on their knees, back straight, head high, shoulders square, and eyes forward. Then we show them how to "Stand Like a Hero." This means getting up without bending over and without placing their hands on the ground. The idea is to stand up with the head up and eyes forward. The kids do this by placing a knee out at a ninety degree angle and then rotating up, using the hips. The end result is that the child is upright and alert with head up, shoulders back, and is ready to move again quickly if required.

CHAPTER 12

TOTAL SAFETY

Now, for the games! True learning comes with repetition. Repetition for kids is boring, so we make repetitive actions into games they can play. We have lots of fun and laughter playing the "Up and Down Game." It reinforces quick, correct movement and mental focus with a series of commands of, "Everybody up!" and, "Everybody down!" A contest or two to see who is the fastest adds to the fun and excitement of the game.

When caught unaware in a potentially dangerous situation, your child needs to be able to move quickly while keeping an eye on the developing situation. If a sexual predator approaches, children need to get up quickly, keep an eye on the approaching individual, and get help. If they are caught in a natural disaster like an earthquake, they need to get up and move quickly and calmly to safety. In other words, the aim of the games is to teach kids to stay calm and take action that moves them into a safer place in threatening situations.

THE POWER OF FOCUS

After a few practice sessions in moving like a hero, the children in our classes are ready to learn how to sharpen their mental focus skills. We teach children as young as four to mentally focus for longer stretches of time. This is paramount in teaching kids to keep themselves safe. We call it the "power of focus."

Whenever a threatening situation is developing, your child needs to be able to spot it. When he spots it, he must focus on it to see the danger and get away from it before it engulfs him. So, we teach the children in our classes to focus. If a child already has this skill, we improve it.

We start with our command of, "Sit like a hero!" We reinforce that with, "Back straight!" then, "Eyes forward!" We ask the kids to pick one spot in front of them and look only at that one spot. Starting with fifteen to twenty seconds at a time, we present this as a game and watch for wandering eyes. We correct them with, "Eyes forward! Focus!"

The fun really starts as we have the kids jump up like a hero, move around, then "Sit like a hero!" with a following command of, "Focus!" Each time they sit, the following focusing exercise becomes a little longer. Over time, most kids can sit for one to two minutes or even more and focus at will. They can turn it on and off at their choosing.

When they really get good with this, we offer a little game, a contest to see who can sit and focus the longest. Again, we must constantly play games and have fun as we build skills.

Mental focus, what we call the power of focus, is developed, practiced, and reinforced in every class in some fashion because of the critical nature of it to child safety.

It is worth saying again:

A CHILD'S ABILITY TO ASSESS A POTENTIALLY DANGEROUS SITUATION DEVELOPING AND GET AWAY FROM IT DEPENDS ON HIS ABILITY TO MENTALLY FOCUS.

CHAPTER 12

TOTAL SAFETY

THE SECRET TO A BETTER FAMILY

Better mental focus in a child is also one of the huge benefits of our Keeping Kids Safe program that translates directly to better families. When your children can focus better, you can talk or communicate with them more easily and get better results from them. Better focus means they will look at you when you speak to them and respond to you more quickly and easily.

It's true! Try it. We actually do these exercises in class to show both parents and children how it works. One, it reinforces our safety lessons. Two, it does make family life better.

Do this:

1. Have the child stand in a relaxed posture.

    - Back straight

    - Legs slightly apart

    - Hands hanging by their side

    - Eyes looking at the ground

2. Stand directly in front of them and ask them to keep looking at the ground.

3. Tell them you are going to give them a list of five different toys that you want them to repeat back to you. For example, a red ball, a pair of gray rollerblades, crayons, a superhero costume, and a Disney edition monopoly game.

4. Have them repeat the list back to you. In most cases, they are unable to repeat the complete list.

5. Now repeat the exercise, but instead of having them look at the floor while you give them the list, have them gaze directly in your eyes.

The results speak for themselves. Whether it's repeating a toy list, cleaning their room, picking up their shoes, or sitting at the dinner table, we get parents into the habit of talking to their kids about important matters in this manner.

PENETRATING LASER EYES

Very few children look people in the eyes, especially people they are talking to. Very few kids look adults directly in the eyes for any reason. Kids are naturally intimidated by larger, older adults. We teach kids in our classes to look anyone they talk to, even adults, right in the eyes. It is a skill kids need to learn. When we teach them this skill, we call it using Hero Laser Eyes.

When a child is confronted with danger from another individual, especially adults, she needs to be able to look that person in the eyes. Looking someone in the eyes does many things for a child. One, it projects confidence that anyone approaching the child can see. Two, it allows the child to clearly assess the intentions of the approaching individual. Three, it gives your child the ability to figure out a safe route out. Four, in some cases, a small child confidently looking at an approaching stranger squarely in the eyes can give the child an extra split second advantage in fleeing a dangerous situation when that stranger is taken by surprise with the intense gaze of a small child.

CHAPTER 12

TOTAL SAFETY

Although your child cannot look anyone in the eye while she is on the computer, she can use this same technique by carefully and intently focusing on the context of the dialogue she is receiving and sending. Looking for "trigger" words that are intended to elicit a certain emotion or response is a good way to focus. Picking up on certain phrases that are intended to guide the conversation in a certain direction or create a certain response and then ignoring them is an example of Online Penetrating Laser Eyes.

HERO POWER VOICE

Another technique we incorporate into our safety techniques is a "Hero Power Voice." This teaches a child to use a strong voice that comes from the abdomen, not the throat. Each child is capable of this type of voice, although he may not have ever used it or even known that he had it.

When kids yell, as with most adults, they yell from their throat. The Hero Power Voice is a yell from their belly. Put your hand on your abdomen, and push out with your stomach muscles. Do it again and huff out a breath with it. Do it one more time, and this time, push out your breath and make a sound with it. It sounds like a deep, "Huh!" More importantly, it comes out with a measure of strength and power. This is the kids' Power Voice.

We practice this by telling the children to, "Bounce Your Voice off the Walls!" Again, it comes from the abdomen, not the throat, and when done correctly, the difference is astonishing. Kids will need to learn to use this voice if they are ever in trouble. It will get people's attention immediately.

Their Online Hero Power Voice comes from their ability to respond, in writing, to something that has offended them or something that they think is wrong or bad. It's their ability to stand up for their beliefs or to refuse to fall prey to someone's threats.

HERO BELLY BRAINS

We teach kids they have two brains, the one in their head and one in their belly. We call the one in the belly the Hero Belly Brain. Kids know how to listen to their Head Brain. They do it everyday, all the time. We teach kids the differences between their two brains and how to listen to their Belly Brain. We teach them that their Belly Brain is always right.

For adults, a Belly Brain is that visceral, gut feeling that is always right. Kids have this gut feeling too, but they need some help in learning how to listen to it and use it to keep themselves safe.

We simply show kids how their Belly Brain works. We teach them to pay attention to it and how to listen to it. More importantly, we show them that listening to it is OK. In doing this, we have to show the kids how their Head Brain can sometimes trick them. We do this by using imagination and storytelling techniques that enable

TOTAL SAFETY

the children to build up a great, exciting tale about a shadow they saw dance across a wall.

It's the same as when kids think monsters are in their bedroom closet or under the bed. We show them how their Head Brain makes these stories up. We then reinforce the Belly Brain as the alarm clock for potentially dangerous situations. We teach the kids to recognize the uneasiness in their stomach without panic, alarm, or worry. We teach them to see potential danger calmly and avoid it with any number of techniques we teach.

When kids tune into their Belly Brain, they are better able to detect uncomfortable situations, questionable adults, and inappropriate behavior. Kids naturally feel uncomfortable when confronted with inappropriate questions or behaviors. We simply show them how to be more aware of it with their Hero Belly Brain.

The kids learn not only to listen to their Belly Brain, but to also go tell Mom and Dad about how they feel and who they were with when they tuned into it.

This Belly Brain also works when your child is online. When children come across something online that makes them feel uncomfortable, their Belly Brain will go off. When they engage in a dialogue that suddenly feels bad, their Belly Brain will go off. Simply teach them to leave the computer and share that information with you as soon as they feel it in their stomach.

DON'T GET PWNed!

THE BEST CIRCLE OF SAFETY

Now that the kids are armed with a lot of the hero traits we want them to have, like confidence, focus, quick movement, and two brains, we begin to subtly weave them into real life situations where kids can use them to keep themselves safe.

At this point, we start to teach actual safety techniques. A good technique to start with is what to do with approaching strangers. When a stranger approaches, any stranger by our Keeping Kids Safe definition, we teach the kids to use a Circle of Safety. A stranger is simply someone you don't know very well. This means you do not know their family, where they live, what kind of car they drive, and you haven't been inside their home and interacted with their family. It is a very simple definition even the youngest of children can understand. A stranger is simply someone the child does not know very well. "Good" or "bad" is irrelevant. All strangers are dealt with in one, simple, easy way with Keeping Kids Safe. When applied with the Circle of Safety concept, a strong safety technique is available to any child.

Many programs teach the Circle of Safety technique. Generally, they teach kids to maintain a Circle of Safety of about eight to ten feet with the child in the center. The child does not allow anyone to enter the circle without turning and running to safety.

The Circle of Safety is a pretty easy idea to teach kids, which makes it a popular technique. Furthermore, the basic Circle of Safety is a good idea in theory—as long as no one moves. This is the problem with most child safety programs that teach a Circle of Safety. In situa-

TOTAL SAFETY

tions where kids are grabbed by predators, no one is standing still. At Keeping Kids Safe, we take the idea of the Circle of Safety one giant step further. We teach a fifteen to twenty feet diameter circle.

Why? It's pretty simple: the standard eight to ten feet Circle of Safety does not work if an adult blitzes in at full speed to grab a kid. Kids need time to react and run at their own speed and still stay ahead of a running adult. The eight to ten feet circle does not give them enough reaction time.

We practice a Circle of Safety with adults charging at the kids. What we find is that the larger circle provides enough distance for even the smallest child to recognize what is happening, turn and run, and evade the grasp of a charging adult. Kids need all the extra help they can get when threatened, and this larger circle gives them that extra bit.

Where does the child run? We teach kids to run and look for someone they can trust, such as:

- A parent
- An adult they know
- A police officer
- A firefighter
- A Mom with children

If the child is in a store or public place and is lost, we teach him to look for a woman with children, a mom, for help. Chances are women with children are moms and will more often help a child lost or in danger than other individuals.

After the children learn what a Circle of Safety is, we teach them how to use it. Kids at Keeping Kids Safe use the Circle of Safety to their advantage by combining it with their power voice and a simple command:

STOP! I'M NOT SUPPOSED TO GET CLOSE TO STRANGERS!

A Circle of Safety by itself is a good thing to teach children. However, the technique is far more powerful when combined with attention-getting tactics. For one thing, a child needs to see a stranger approaching. As a stranger gets to the edge of the Circle of Safety, we teach kids to raise their hand in a "halt" gesture and in their Super Hero Voice say, "STOP!" The adult or approaching stranger will usually stop and ask, "Why?" The child then says, "I'm not allowed to get close to strangers," again in their strong Super Hero Voice.

If the stranger continues toward the child, the child knows to turn and run away and look for someone for help. If the stranger simply has a question like, "I'm looking for the hospital," she can still ask the child from a distance. The fifteen to twenty feet Circle of Safety allows for normal conversation. Also, good strangers will recognize what the child is doing and move away, as most responsible people will do, when this happens.

Kids are taught in Keeping Kids Safe to never let any stranger into their Circle of Safety. If an adult persists in entering their circle, we teach them to turn and run. When a child turns and runs from her Circle of Safety, she needs to get the attention of someone who will

TOTAL SAFETY

help them immediately. We teach kids to yell "FIRE!" whenever they get into trouble.

Fire? Yes, "FIRE!" for many reasons. One, kids are always yelling when they play. One of their favorite things to yell when playing is "help!" They also tend to yell "help!" in very high-pitched, throaty voices.

Adults and other family members quickly learn to ignore these false cries for help. If a child yells "help!" and really means it, chances are he will be ignored. He will not get the help he needs when he needs it.

We teach kids to yell, "FIRE!" when they are in need of real help. The word "fire" gets anyone's attention immediately. Even if it is yelled in a high–pitched, throaty voice it will get people's attention.

The idea behind these simple yet effective techniques is to have one, clear-cut rule that kids, even the youngest kids, can follow. That, is, kids are to keep a Circle of Safety around themselves with any stranger. When a bad stranger (one who ignores the child's attempt to stay distant) invades the Circle of Safety, a child is to turn and run while yelling, "FIRE!" for help.

Your child's online Circle of Safety is dependent on your child recognizing who online is a "stranger." A stranger online or offline is simply someone your child doesn't know very well. "Very well" means that person has been in your home, interacted with your family, shared a meal, and so on. It also means you know where they live and who their friends are and basically have a relationship with them.

DON'T GET PWNed!

HOW TO PROTECT YOUR CHILD ONLINE

We teach kids that when talking with strangers, they should never tell them anything that is none of the strangers' business, namely personal information. If your child is engaged in an online conversation with someone she doesn't know very well, and that person is asking personal questions, your child should respond by telling the stranger that she doesn't know them well enough to answer those questions. If that line of questioning persists, she should then come to you.

CHAPTER SUMMARY

- From the time they step through that door, we call all of our students heroes. It is a teaching tool.

- Using heroes as examples is an attention-getting technique that gets us the results we want in teaching kids to keep themselves safe.

- We teach kids how to:

  √ "Sit Like a Hero"

  √ "Stand Like a Hero"

  √ Use a "Hero Power Voice"

  √ Listen to their "Hero Belly Brain."

- We teach kids how to use an expanded "Circle of Safety."

- We teach kids how to yell, "Fire!" when they are in trouble.

- We teach kids how to deal with strangers, any stranger, for total safety.

- We play games with the kids in our classes to reinforce the safety techniques we teach them.

- When in a potentially dangerous situation, your child needs to be able to move quickly while keeping an eye on the developing situation. If a sexual predator approaches him, your child needs to get up swiftly, keep an eye on the approaching individual, and leave the area quickly and safely.

- A child's ability to assess a potentially dangerous situation she must get away from depends on her ability to focus.

- Better mental focus in a child is also one of the huge benefits of our Keeping Kids Safe program that carries over to better family communication.

- If a child is in a store or public place and is lost, we teach him to look for a woman with children, a mom, for help.

ABOUT KEEPING KIDS SAFE

REVEALING THE SECRETS BEHIND THE PROGRAM

Keeping Kids Safe is about safe kids and better families. It works most effectively when parents embrace the concepts as adults and bring it to their entire family with their parenting skills. In short, it's a way of life.

For the last twenty years, we have been developing and teaching the Keeping Kids Safe program. We have found unequivocally that if you focus on the kids, then focus on the parents, getting them both to take on the challenge of being the best human beings they can be, then and only then can we teach them real, effective, lifelong safety techniques. We know if we do not follow this sequence, the safety of the child is always in question.

Our program has got to be about kids being able to keep themselves safe. Most children are safe when Mom or Dad is around. It is all about kids who find themselves alone and without Mom and Dad for any reason.

Our extensive backgrounds in psychology, personal safety, martial arts, and community- based teaching programs have allowed us to combine a number of areas of expertise into one very effective series of safety classes. We even have specialty safety classes that cover a range of age groups.

DON'T GET PWNed!

HOW TO PROTECT YOUR CHILD ONLINE

Our expertise allows us to provide programs for parents with children spanning a wide range of ages: expectant moms, parents with toddlers, elementary age children, teens, and even college co-eds. There is also a Special Needs Recreational program that is very close to our hearts.

It is our approach to safety that is unique. We teach a serious subject like personal safety in a fun, entertaining, and exciting way. A lot of what we teach you may know. A lot of what we teach you may not know. We will change that.

A good part of our philosophy of safety is controversial. To that we say, "good!" We think parents are instrumental in their children's safety. Their ability to parent from a positive, encouragement-based perspective is crucial for developing great kids. Some parents need to wake up to this idea, and we shake them awake.

We tell parents in the first class that we are going to say things they may not agree with. We are going to say things that will make them uncomfortable. Many parents in our classes like what they hear, and some do not. We are very clear and upfront with our ideas on keeping kids safe. If a parent is not committed 100 percent to our program, it will not work for them or their child. They are wasting their time.

The first thing we tell parents is that they are responsible for their child's safety. We tell them real safety begins at home. We tell them real safety is reinforced at home by Mom and Dad. We tell parents directly that they have to be the best people they can be in order to teach their kids to be the best they can be.

ABOUT KEEPING KIDS SAFE

REVEALING THE SECRETS BEHIND THE PROGRAM

Talking to the parents is how we start, but we relate directly to the kids, too. We engage the children and let them tell us what they think about a number of subjects we broach. In doing so, we listen carefully to their words. In responding, we use the exact same words the children use since they understand what those words mean. We also use the words in the same manner the kids do. Using the same words in the same way enables us to connect with the kids almost instantly.

We also carefully sequence information in ways we know kids will absorb and retain it. We know how to teach kids so they learn effectively and quickly. We introduce certain concepts and terms in the first few weeks to both parents and kids and then subtly weave concepts together with a series of exercises and games that aid and reinforce the learning process for the kids.

While we teach the children themselves, we work with the families as a total unit. Whatever we work on needs to be reinforced and practiced at home. This includes the confidence-building and focus-building techniques. This is why we say we have a secondary focus, which is to make families better by learning and practicing safety together.

Kids need the security and companionship of a group, a unit. We believe this unit should be a family, a solid, positive, nurturing family. We simply accent the family for greater child safety.

After all, we are just like you. Parents concerned about their kids. We started with a single thought to help one child. Today, we are simply two people with a laser-focused mission.

DON'T GET PWNed!

HOW TO PROTECT YOUR CHILD ONLINE

Our MISSION is to teach twenty million kids by 2010 to keep themselves safe.

Our PURPOSE is to benefit kids directly by developing the core values of confidence, respect, honesty, integrity, and dignity to carry with them for a lifetime of safety.

Our VISION is to create a global community with like-minded individuals willing to take on the responsibility of mentoring kids with our purpose and core values.

ABOUT THE AUTHORS

THE RICHES OF A SINGLE THOUGHT

C hild-safety experts are not born. As authors, consultants, speakers, and trainers, we have accumulated our expertise and knowledge over many years. It began, however, with a single thought.

A single thought is powerful. A single thought produces riches beyond imagination. Keeping Kids Safe started with a single thought by one man who desired to make a difference in the world. Amazing things happened, riches for all, by following that single thought with action. Preston Jones is the creator and developer of Keeping Kids Safe. The program began as a labor of love intended to make a positive difference in the lives of children and their families. It started with Preston agreeing to help a single family become safer following an idea, a single thought, and a desire to help. A mother with a special needs son with behavioral issues approached Preston for help after she attended one of his morning meditation sessions at a weekend retreat. She thought the calming effect might help her son if Preston worked with him one-on-one. Preston agreed, and Keeping Kids Safe was started.

Today, Keeping Kids Safe is a culmination of thirty years of combined experience, expertise, and constant dedication by Preston Jones and Joyce Jackson. They are continually evaluating and improving the program as the world we live in changes. Their ultimate goal is to offer every child the opportunity to grow up feeling safe and secure and confident in themselves.

Preston honed his approach to child safety through a prolific thirty-year career focusing on personal safety for a variety of age groups and organizations. From Keeping Kids Safe to police and security departments, his expertise has helped thousands learn to keep themselves safe.

It wasn't always that way. Preston grew up in a dysfunctional household in central Missouri, the only son of six children. With an alcoholic father and an overbearing mother, Preston often bore the brunt of his alcoholic father's rage. This coupled with the fact that his family was poor resulted in Preston developing low self-esteem and virtually no self-confidence during his younger years. As a result, Preston developed a severe stuttering impediment when he was eleven years old. For the next three years he was the focus of ridicule from his schoolmates and peers. However, all this changed when his family moved to a neighboring community when he was fourteen.

On his first day at his new school, he overheard a classmate make a positive comment about him. This was the first time he could remember anyone saying anything positive about him. To this day he remembers the tremendous impact that one simple comment made on his life. Although he didn't realize it at the time, this experience was to become the driving force behind Keeping Kids Safe and Preston's mission of helping kids and families become the best they can be.

After serving six years in the United States Air Force, Preston enrolled at Missouri State University and received his Bachelor's degree in Psychology. After moving to California, he continued his studies by enrolling in a graduate program at John F. Kennedy University. Realizing the opportunities California offered, Preston took an entrepreneur approach to business, only to fail in two different attempts. Reflecting on his psychology background, he began to realize that most of his poor choices were a result of his childhood experiences.

Vowing not to repeat past mistakes, Preston put the past in perspective and took full responsibility for his future and created Keeping Kids Safe in the format it exists in today. His devotion to the subject of child safety and kids being given the chance to be the best they can be stems from being a former police officer, Air Force veteran, martial arts fifth degree black belt, university student of psychology and parapsychology, and most of all, a father of two daughters.

Preston's expertise goes further than this. In 1991, he was approached by the city of Walnut Creek, California to begin an adaptive martial arts program for children and adults with special needs. A few years later, the position of program coordinator in the Walnut Creek's Specialized Recreation Department became vacant, and he stepped in to fill it when asked to do so.

Since taking over the program, Preston and the Department have received numerous awards from the city of Walnut Creek, the Developmental Disabilities Council of Contra Costa and Alameda counties, and the California Senate. The highly praised program continues today.

Preston's programs and seminars are sought out by public and professional organizations throughout the San Francisco bay area.

His expertise extends to include defensive tactics, baton training, handcuffing techniques, and small arms firearm training for police officers and private security companies.

Today Preston lives in the San Francisco Bay area with his wife Sandra and two daughters, Samantha and Olivia.

Joyce Jackson is also a part of Keeping Kids Safe. She is a child safety expert and co-owner of Keeping Kids Safe. She first became familiar with the program when she enrolled her four–year-old son in a Keeping Kids Safe class. Shortly thereafter, she began learning the program philosophy and techniques and began assisting in the classes. From there she began teaching them and creating a business partnership with Preston.

Despite being the owner of a design and consulting firm in the San Francisco Bay area, a marathon runner, a martial arts black belt, and a mom, Joyce views herself as someone just like anyone else who has faced the struggles of everyday life. Joyce's personal goal is the same as that of Keeping Kids Safe, that is, to teach twenty million kids by 2010 to keep themselves safe.

Joyce grew up in the western suburbs of Chicago in an all-too-familiar dysfunctional family. Her family lived in a blue collar neighborhood where alcoholism and spousal abuse were the norm. Joyce's father traveled as a salesman, and his philandering ways affected the entire family. Her mother escaped most of the time into alcoholism and the sinking quicksand of acute mental depression.

Joyce found herself alone throughout childhood and distinctly different from other girls her age. Her natural athletic abilities coupled with an inner unspoken drive to "make a difference in this world" constantly drove her into waters that were "off limits to women" at the time.

She would have surely followed in her older sister's footsteps of alcoholism and drug abuse if it were not for a junior high school teacher who took her aside one afternoon after she had found herself in the principals' office once again. He said, "You know, you are absolutely brilliant. If you would just stop goofing off and take yourself seriously, you could be anything you want to be. You could even get out of this place."

This was the first time in twelve years anyone had said anything positive or encouraging to her. After the shock of the discussion sank in, Joyce began to slowly realize she could head in a direction different from her family, neighborhood, or friends. To this day, she remembers and is thankful for the tremendous impact that one individual, Richard Cerwyn, has made on her life. Later Joyce would realize this experience was the one event that convinced her that one person can influence and change the world.

As Joyce's life evolved, she became ostracized by her family. Over the years, with the help of other key individuals and spurred on by a tenacious personal mission to improve herself and the world, Joyce escaped the destructiveness of her family environment.

She is no stranger to action as she enjoyed a prolific twenty-five year career as a licensed and practicing architect. Prior to Keeping Kids Safe, she spent twelve years as a business partner and co-owner of a design and consulting firm in the San Francisco Bay Area. Her strategic planning and execution skills have helped bring Keeping Kids Safe into every home across the globe.

Her instrumental role with Keeping Kids Safe, coupled with a tenacious persistence to keeping as many kids as possible safe and secure, has catapulted her into the forefront of child safety with Preston Jones. Her personal skills allow her to bring phenomenal drive and energy to building strong relationships with strategic partners and organizing and accessing groups that span the globe to keep as many kids around the world as safe as possible.

She is proud to be a partner, but more importantly, a friend of Preston Jones. She lives in the San Francisco Bay Area with her husband Robert and two sons, Zachary and Nathaniel. Keeping Kids Safe continues to empower children to be the best they can be. If kids can walk down the street with their shoulders back, heads held high, eyes bright, and minds aware of their environment, they are less of a target for predators.

Keeping Kids Safe is about safe kids and better families. Preston and Joyce, with the help of their program, make a difference in people's lives. They do it with their unique approach that incorporates the parents into the process of teaching their children to keep themselves safer. You can now be a welcomed member of the Keeping Kids Safe family. It is timely, effective, simple, and filled with common sense to help you and your child.

Preston and Joyce will help you mentor your kids. They will enable you to keep them safer today than they were yesterday. By being a Keeping Kids Safe family member and carrying out the principles of teaching your kids to keep themselves safe, you will give them safety skills for a lifetime. The precept of "Don't give them a fish, teach them how to fish" is what Keeping Kids Safe is all about.

FURTHER READING FROM KEEPING KIDS SAFE

HOW TO PROTECT YOUR CHILD
FROM SEXUAL PREDATORS

H*ow to Protect Your Child from Sexual Predators* has been recognized as the preeminent text for developing the next generation of safe kids by the nation's most prestigious child safety professionals. This #1 Bestseller has been recommended by Dr. Arline Kerman, PhD, JD; Cynthia Tiano and Dr. Max Vogt; John DiLemme, motivational speaker; Dr. Nikolas Makhoul, MD; Heidi Nabert, noted sexual abuse survivor; Leadership Trainer Jason Oman; and many, many more.

How to Protect Your Child from Sexual Predators has won all of this support because it is the first and only safety How To guide on the market that is (1) intended for parents, grandparents, or anyone who cares about kids; (2) written in easy-to-understand language; (3) structured for quick access to information; (4) presented in a simple reference guide format that anyone can use immediately to make a difference in their child's safety. In all, the book is praised for its no-nonsense approach to child safety in today's twenty-first century world.

DON'T GET PWNed!

HOW TO PROTECT YOUR CHILD ONLINE

HEALTHY KIDS, SAFER KIDS

Ultimate twenty-first-century safety meets good eating habits. This groundbreaking book marries the ideas of confidence-building for safety with good nutrition and health habits for safer, healthier kids. Healthier kids are more energetic and alert. Healthy kids are naturally less of a target for any kind of childhood threat, from bullies at school to predators prowling the neighborhood. Coming in late 2008, get this quick-start guide to healthier kids including exercise, drug safety, and healthy eating.

CONFIDENT KIDS, SAFER KIDS

We all know confident kids are naturally less of a target for any kind of childhood predator. We also know confidence is a foundation for a lifetime of happiness, health, and safety in today's changing world. This step-by-step How To guide will add to your arsenal of parenting skills that provide you with the family you want—full of happy, confident kids who grow into happy and confident adults.

BECAUSE "I SAID SO!" DOESN'T WORK ANYMORE

Parenting meets twenty-first-century challenges. This guide for parents on parenting safe children for a lifetime gets right to the heart of the issue: parents are responsible for creating a solid foundation of confidence, health, and safety for their kids. This book demystifies the secrets to great kids. Get the skills you need, or take your parenting skills to the next level. Due to be out in late 2008.

FURTHER READING

"YOU DON'T TRUST ME!" IS BUSTED

Finally, a book by teens for teens that "shoots straight" about personal safety. Dating, friends, peers, parents, and being online and in chat rooms are just some of the topics this great book covers. Growing up in today's twenty-first century world is a different experience from when we were teenagers. Read the scoop from the kids themselves. Due to be out early 2009.

ENDNOTES

1. David Finkelhor et al., "Online Victimization of Youth: Five Years Later," (National Center for Missing & Exploited Children, 2006), 7, 8, 33.

2. Amanda Lenhart, "Cyberbullying and Online Teens" (The Pew Internet and American Life Project, June 27, 2007).

3. Dr Michael Carr-Gregg, "Cyberbullying," (National Coalition Against Bullying and Girlfriend Magazine, The Australian, April 20, 2006), 17.

4. M. Fleming et al., "Educational Forum on Adolescent Health: Youth Bullying," (paper presented at the Chicago meeting of the American Medical Association, 2002).

5. Mark Anderson et al., "School-associated Violent Deaths in the United States, 1994-1999," Journal of the American Medical Association. (2001):286:2695-2702.

6. Andrea Cohn et al., "Bullying: Facts for Schools and Parents," (presented at the National Association of School Psychologists, October 7, 2003).

7. Federal Bureau of Investigation, "Financial Crimes Report to the Public Fiscal Year 2006, October 1, 2005–September 30, 2006," http://www.fbi.gov/.

8. Technology & Democracy Project, "U.S. Internet Traffic Projected to Grow 50-Fold by 2015, New Study Shows Required

Network Expansion Could Cost $100 Billion Over Next Five Years," http://www.Discovery.org/, January 29, 2008.

9. Bill Gates, Craig Mundie, "Microsoft Government Leaders Forum-Asia 2007," (transcript of remarks by Bill Gates, Chairman, Microsoft Corporation Craig Mundie, Chief Research and Strategy Officer, Microsoft Corporation, April 19, 2007).

10. Grant Gross, "Study: Internet Could Run Out of Capacity in Two Years, Nemertes Research Group has published a study indicating that consumer and corporate demands on the Internet could outstrip capacity very soon," IDG News Service, http://www.InfoWorld.com, November 19, 2007.

11. Federal Bureau of Investigation, "Travelers' Advisory Beware of Online Child Predators," http://www.FBI.gov/, December 12, 2005.

12. MySpace, "MySpace and Attorneys General Announce Joint Effort to Promote Industry-Wide Internet Safety Principle, Attorneys General Praise MySpace Safety Efforts and Call for Broad Adoption; Endeavor to Include New Protections for Teens and Tools for Parents," NewsCorporation Press Release, http://www.Newscorp.com/, January 15, 2008.

13. ibid

14. Jimmy P. Miller, "Developing a profile for sexual deviants nearly impossible," The New Jersey Express-Times, Monday, February 23, 2004.

15. Federal Bureau of Investigation, "A Parent's Guide to Internet

Safety," http://www.fbi.gov/publications/pguide/pguidee.htm/.

16. Ravi Agrawal, "Social Networking Fuels New Web Boom," http://www.cnn.com/, October 3, 2006.

17. Tobi Elkin, "Just an Online Minute ... Teens, Tweens, and Cell Phones" MediaPost Publications, March 10, 2005.

18. Laura Petrecca, "Cell Phone Marketers Calling All Preteens," http://www.usatoday.com/, September 5, 2005.

19. "Community Based Sex Offender Treatment Program," John Howard Society of Alberta, http://www.johnhoward.ab.ca/PUB/C18.htm#sex/,1997.

20. Josh Lanier, "Former Teacher Charged with Sexual Misconduct," Independent Tribune, http://www.independenttribune.com/, February 22, 2008.

21. Associated Press, "Police Arrest 'MySpace' Predator," Des Moines (AP), http://www.kcrg.com/news/local/15540222.html/, Feb 12, 2008.

22. "Father-of-four Jailed for Grooming Schoolgirl," Grantham Journal, http://www.granthamjournal.co.uk/news/Fatheroffour-jailed-for-grooming-schoolgirl.3760565.jp/, February 2008.

23. Jenny Michael, "Girl Says She Was Coerced into Sending Photo," The Bismark Tribune, http://www.bismarcktribune.com/articles/2008/02/08/news/local/148392.txt/, February 8, 2008.

24. Will Safer, "Another MySpace Predator Caught Going after Children," Switch, http://www.switched.com/2008/01/15/another-myspace-predator-caught/, January 15, 2008.

25. Abbas Abedi, "Learn Some Important Basics of Body Language," Health Guidance, http://www.healthguidance.org/entry/5420/1/Learn-Some-Important-Basics-Of-Body-Language.html/.

26. John Rosemond, *Because I Said So!: A Collection of 366 Insightful and Thought-Provoking Reflections on Parenting and Family Life* (Kansas City, Mo: Andrews and McMeel, a Universal Press Syndicate Compnay,1996), 64.

BONUS
FREE INTERNET
SAFETY TOOL KIT

A $39.95 VALUE!

Do You Want The Secrets To Your Child's Internet Safety Instantly?

Now you can have them . . . and in plain, simple language. . . immediately.

GO TO: WWW.INTERNETSAFETYOFFER.COM

For your Free INTERNET SAFETY TOOLKIT.

We've traveled the country asking parents just like you, what your major concerns are about your child's internet safety. We know you want to dissolve your fears about your child online.

NOW YOU CAN DO SOMETHING ABOUT IT!

Get your FREE *Internet Safety Tool Kit* INSTANTLY!

- Instant Chat Room Safety Secrets Audio
- Handling Cyberbullies with Ease Audio
- The Keys to Keeping Your Kids from Stumbling onto Inappropriate Websites

DON'T GET PWNed!

HOW TO PROTECT YOUR CHILD ONLINE

- The Easy Steps to Keeping Your Computer Safe from Cyber Threats
- Special Discount Coupon for our #1 Bestselling book *How to Protect Your Child From Sexual Predators*
- Chat Room Safety Secrets QUICK TIPS Card
- Chat Room Shorthand Definitions QUICK GUIDE
- The 7 Pitfalls Online to Avoid
- The Keys to Keeping Your Teenager Safer Online
- A 1/2 Hour Phone Consultation with Preston Jones and Joyce Jackson

GO TO: WWW.INTERNETSAFETYOFFER.COM
All INSTANTLY!
This is a $39.95 value, yours FREE and

more in our Internet Safety Tool Kit.

GO TO: WWW.INTERNETSAFETYOFFER.COM
Take Our Safety Tips Wherever You Go!

THE BELLY BRAIN PODCASTS
…the A,B,C,'s of safety for busy parents
Rated by Parents Everywhere

BONUS